Native American Perspectives on Literature and History

American Indian Literature and Critical Studies Series

Gerald Vizenor and Louis Owens, General Editors

Native American Perspectives on Literature and History

Edited by Alan R. Velie

University of Oklahoma Press
Norman and London

K

ISBN 0-8061-2785-6

Native American Perspectives on Literature and History is Volume 19 in the American Indian Literature and Critical Studies Series.

This volume consists of essays previously published in the journal *Genre* 25, no. 4 (1994).

The paper in this book meets the guidelines for permanence and durability of the Committee on Production Guidelines for Book Longevity of the Council on Library Resources, Inc. ∞

1 2 3 4 5 6 7 8 9 10

CONTENTS

INTRODUCTION

ALAN R. VELIE, UNIVERSITY OF OKLAHOMA

GERALD VIZENOR, UNIVERSITY OF CALIFORNIA, BERKELEY

This issue is devoted to American Indian perspectives. The articles, by both tribal members and nonIndians, examine how questions of identity have a bearing on the way Indians construct narratives in fiction and history.

Indians have been misunderstood by others since Columbus mistook the Caribs for natives of India. Europeans were determined to conquer and control the New World. Their knowledge was flawed by their obsessions. Many colonial Americans believed that the Indians who did not convert to Christianity were Devil worshippers. As one Puritan put it, the war between whites and Indians was a holy war between the forces of God and the Devil, a

> "quarrel . . . as ancient as Adams time, propagated from that old enmity between the Seede of the Woman, and the Seede of the Serpent, who was the grand signior of this war." (Slotkin 77)

The concept of Indian as other, the evil shadow who opposed the occidental persona in not only popular literature, but even the work of writers like Mark Twain and Nathaniel Hawthorne, persisted throughout the 19th and early 20th Century. When the dime novel gave way to the western movie, Indians remained the villains of choice, and it wasn't until the Civil Rights movement brought a measure of sensitivity to America that Indians were treated as anything but stereotypes, either bloodthirsty villain, or noble savage, the faithful Indian companion, Squanto or Tonto.

In 1968 Scott Momaday published *House Made of Dawn*, beginning what has come to be known as "the American Indian Literary Renaissance." Few people knew about the Indian writers who had published before Momaday—D'arcy Mc-

Nickle and John Joseph Mathews, for instance. In the past generation James Welch, Leslie Silko, Louise Erdrich and Gerald Vizenor, among others, have received a good deal of recognition for their fiction. This has spurred a body of criticism, mostly by white academics. Although most of the critics would describe themselves as "friends of the Indian," their analyses have often been narrow and imperceptive. In most cases the critics simply applied western aesthetic standards to the works they discussed; their interpretations were often inadequate or inappropriate to the material. In attempting to understand the culture of the writers and their subjects, the critics usually depended on the works of white anthropologists. Sometimes, in an attempt to understand the culture of the writer the critics insisted in seeing the works purely in a tribal context, ignoring the fact that the writers were thoroughly imbued with middle class American culture as well as experiencing that of their own tribes.

In this issue James Ruppert explores the bicultural nature of Indian writers, and discusses the strategies they use in addressing several audiences: their tribe, other Indians, and other Americans. In "Mediation in Contemporary Native American Writing" Ruppert discusses how Indians participate in both tribal and mainstream American culture. Employing the theories of M. M. Bahktin, Julia Kristeva and Hayden White, among others, Ruppert shows how Indian writers act as mediators between Indian and Anglo cultural traditions; that is, how they use the epistemological frameworks of the traditions to "illuminate and enrich each other."

Helen Jaskoski uses the term "autoethnography" to describe Indian historical writing. In particular she discusses Ottawa writer Andrew Blackbird's account of a smallpox epidemic. Autoethnographic writings were intended for both whites and Indians. They attempted to correct fallacious views of Indians, the result of white prejudice and ignorance, and to preserve Indian traditions.

Smallpox was a deadly weapon of war that the whites employed against Indians, and smallpox stories constitute a distinct Indian genre. In Blackbird's account the disease is sent to the Indians as a gift enclosed in a wad of cotton contained in the innermost of a set of nested boxes.

Often, given tribal conceptions of science and medicine, smallpox stories seem fanciful or allegorical—e.g., the disease is pictured as a deadly rider—but Jaskoski makes a convincing case that Blackbird's account is literally correct. The smallpox was sent in the fashion normally used for inoculation, only in this case the dose was deadly.

Kimberly Blaeser writes about the way that "history *forms* native writing"; that is, how the "consciousness of historical continuum is sounded in the voice of native writers." She discusses how Indian writers reappropriate their history, regaining possession of the stories of their land and their people. In particular she focusses on three writers, Carter Revard, Gerald Vizenor and Gordon Henry, who use humor to "force a reconsideration of the processes and powers of historical reckoning" to the end of bringing the reader an "imaginative reevaluation of history."

According to Blaeser, Revard, Vizenor and Henry differ sharply from those historians who consider themselves objective: that is, who believe they produce a narrative they consider true and unbiased. Revard *et al* are aware of the conflicting nature of historical versions, and play with the possibilities of diverse accounts.

Robert Warrior explores the ideas of Vine Deloria, the Sioux writer who has been the leading political philosopher in the Indian community for the past three decades. Deloria calls for a return to traditional tribal religions as a means of asserting tribal sovereignty and gaining autonomy and power. The reaffirmation of traditional beliefs is necessary to encourage and empower Indians who have been told that their ancestors were barbaric pagans. But, Deloria realizes that traditions are living things, and that Indians cannot simply dress in beads and feathers and live as if it were still 1850—something that many whites as well as Indians believe appropriate behavior.

Warrior discusses Deloria's reaction to the events at Wounded Knee in 1973, where Indian activists put into action some of the ideas Deloria had been preaching, but in a way Deloria found repugnant to a large degree. But although Wounded Knee was a disappointment for Deloria, the actions of the AIM members who participated in the takeover there struck a chord in the Indian community, particularly among the most disenfranchised. The major question for Deloria is how to wed tradition with practical politics: how to eschew the romantic radicalism and resultant confrontation that often results from emphasis on ethnic differences, and genuinely empower tribes.

Robert Berner writes about the role of myth in American history, particularly as it applies to the place and image of Indians. He notes the effect of myth on language: how traditionally in America an engagement is a "battle" if whites win, and a "massacre" if the Indians prevail. Berner also takes the academic left to task for their loose use of "genocide" and "holocaust."

Berner's most important point is the interrelationship of white and Indian culture. His examples are Squanto, the Pawtuxet who taught the Pilgrims to use fish as fertilizer, and Black Elk, the Sioux shaman who became a Christian. Squanto, the legendary figure whose story is told to schoolchildren every Thanksgiving, had spent years in Europe, and perhaps was merely passing on a trick he had learned there.

Black Elk, whose memoir *Black Elk Speaks* is one of the most widely read biographies in America, is known as a tribal seer, a man who had an extraordinary religious vision. The book ends with the massacre at Wounded Knee, and the capitulation of the Sioux. Although Black Elk lived for sixty years after Wounded Knee, and converted to Catholicism, John Neihardt, the man who put together *Black Elk Speaks*—a sort of "as told to" arrangement—chose not to let readers know that Black Elk had become Christian, as if the fact were shameful, some sort of betrayal. Berner raises questions about whether Black Elk renounced his earlier religion, or simply added his new faith to his old one, the source of his vision. Berner's point is that ethnicity is a complex matter in America. People like Neihardt deliberately make it a simple one, generally to make a political point to serve the general politics of publishing at the time.

Alan Velie uses Hayden White's analyses of historical writing to examine two very different historical novels, James Welch's *Fools Crow*, and Gerald Vizenor's *The Heirs of Columbus. Fools Crow* employs the conventions of the traditional historical novel. He does what Georg Lukács praised Walter Scott for: he delivers a plausible recreation of a world long gone. Welch, like Scott, uses dollops of exotic language; he scatters Blackfeet words and hybrid Blackfeet-English phrases ("he would hunt the white big head . . . through the moon of the falling leaves"). The effect is what James calls an "air of verisimilitude": the reader feels he is living with the Blackfeet in the 19th Century.

Velie argues that Gerald Vizenor chooses a totally different set of conventions; his novel is a postmodern fantasy. In it Columbus is an Indian whose heirs establish a utopia funded by high stakes bingo. For all its comic exuberance, the book raises serious questions about history and the sources of narrative. Implicitly it puts into question the notion that the standard sorts of verisimilar history are "objective," to use the term that Lukács applies to Scott.

In "Boxcar Babies" Kurt Peters describes a settlement of Laguna Indians from New Mexico who lived in the Santa Fe railroad yard in Richmond, California from the 1920s to the 1980s. The railroad had an agreement to provide jobs to the Lagunas, and provided housing in the form of converted boxcars. An African-American observer described the facilities as "pitiful" and "pathetic," but Peters found on interviewing the Lagunas that they were pleased with the accommodations and proud of their association with the railroad. Peters concludes that the Lagunas were able to maintain their cultural heritage in California, and construct their community as colonies of their New Mexico pueblo. They resisted being urbanized into the East Bay community, and made it clear to the African-American observer that they resented the intrusion of well-meaning outsiders.

In "Vizenor's Shadow Plays: Mediations and Multiplicities of Power," Juana Rodriguez applies Foucauldian ideas of power to analyze Vizenor's journalistic account of the crime and punishment of Sioux murderer Thomas White Hawk. Vizenor writes with the goal of getting White Hawk's death penalty reduced. He succeeds; ultimately White Hawk was sentenced to life without parole.

As Vizenor depicts him, White Hawk is an odd sort of Oedipus. In killing jewelry salesman James Yeado, and raping Yeado's wife, White Hawk is symbolically killing the foster father who abused him sexually, and having sex with the man's wife. As Rodriguez sees it, Vizenor is constructing a story out of several preexisting narratives: the colonial narrative in which White Hawk is "committing an act of treason against the purity of the white social order"; the cultural nationalist narrative in which White Hawk is a "victim of the hegemonic powers that seek to destroy him"; and the white feminist narrative which identifies White Hawk as an abuser of women.

In "Native American Indian Identities," Gerald Vizenor writes about the elusive claims of Indian identity by selected writers. He argues that both public and private identities are earned in a communal context, in a family, in a name, but not by mere commercial or aesthetic adoption. Recently writer Jamake Highwater, with no Indian "blood" whatever, claimed to be Blackfeet, and established a reputation as an expert on Indian affairs. Bill Trogdon, with a trace of Siouan genes in his veins, changed his name to William Least Heat-Moon, and wrote a bestseller. Kenneth Lincoln makes constant reference to his adoption by the Oglala. Vizenor analyzes the reasons for the simulations of Indian identity, or as he sometimes calls it "postindian identity."

WORK CITED

Slotkin, Richard. *Regeneration Through Violence: The Mythology of the American Frontier.* Middletown, Conn:, Wesleyan University Press, 1973.

MEDIATION IN CONTEMPORARY NATIVE AMERICAN WRITING

James Ruppert, University of Alaska, Fairbanks

Contemporary Native American writers are in an innovative position full of potential. As participants in two cultural traditions, their art is patterned by discursive acts of mediation at many levels. By mediation, I mean an artistic and conceptual standpoint, constantly flexible, which uses the epistemological frameworks of Native American and Western cultural traditions to illuminate and enrich each other.[1] In working toward an understanding of their texts, it is more useful to see these writers, not as between two cultures (a romantic and victimist perspective) but as participants in two rich cultural traditions. While some may say these writers are apologists for one side or the other, or that their texts inhabit a no-man's land, a mediational approach explores how their texts create a dynamic that brings differing cultural codes into confluence to reinforce and recreate the structures of human life—the self, community, spirit, and the world we perceive. Through their mediating position, the writers are "protecting and celebrating the cores of cultures left in the wake of catastrophe" (Erdrich, "Where" 23).

They may bust European American stereotypes, create cultural criticism of the dominant society, and make manifest the crimes of the past, but their mediational goals direct them toward more Native concerns with nurturing survival, continuance, and continual reemergence of cultural identity. As Gerald Vizenor has written in his own inimitable style, "Native American Indian literatures are

---

[1] This use of mediation should be distinguished from Franz Stanzel's use of the term "Mittelbarkeit" usually translated as "mediacy". Stanzel is concerned with a survey of the interaction of person, perspective, and mode as they determine how a narrator functions as a mediator between the author and the reader. My analysis seeks to plot the cognitive ground of a specific field of narrative.

tribal discourse, more discourse. The oral and written narratives are language games, comic discourse rather than mere responses to colonialist demands or social science theories" ("Introduction" 4). For many scholars only the social tragedy has been important in contemporary Native American Literature. The works function, according to such scholars, to represent the colonization of Native peoples. However, the texts clearly reject victimized literary interpretations.

It is all too obvious that contemporary Native American fiction, poetry, and drama conform to many Western expectations and present characters who can be understood in terms of Western psychology and sociology. But James Clifford suggests that even our conceptions of cultural continuity may be inadequate to the understanding of contemporary Native American experience. Thus in texts by contemporary Native writers, "Metaphors of continuity and 'survival' do not account for complex historical processes of appropriation, compromise, subversion, masking, invention, and revival" (338). But perhaps most difficult and potentially illuminating can be the realizations of Native goals and tribal discourse which coexist with more Western goals in the text and texture of these works. An exploration of how Hyemeyohsts Storm's *Seven Arrows* engages contemporary Euro-American social discourse of the 1960s might be as revealing as a discussion of Chippewa vision discourse in Gerald Vizenor's *Darkness in Saint Louis Bearheart*.

Much necessary and solid research has been done establishing the cultural references of contemporary Native American Literature. But historical and textual scholars have combined with more anthropologically-minded scholars to downplay the contemporary literary discourse in the texts. Too often the attitude has been that to participate in the text, one must read an anthropologist first, turning the critical activity into what Andrew Wiget calls, "a kind of shadow anthropology" ("Identity" 259). Some sociological reactionary criticism has even explored the texts solely in terms of how they responded to American attitudes toward assimilation. No scholar has explored in depth the question of multiple audiences, and the attempts to apply current literary theory or comparativist approaches have often been discounted by reviewers. A mediational methodology is designed to appreciate contemporary Native American literary works as bi-cultural texts patterning an active encounter with distinct audiences.

In discussing Native American literature, Paula Gunn Allen directs our attention to the mediational quality of contemporary texts and to some of their Native directions. She perceives contemporary Native American novels as becoming increasingly concerned with tribal and urban life. Though they overlay Western narrative plotting, they are essentially ritualistic in approach, structure, theme, symbol, and significance. They "rely on native rather than non-Indian forms, themes, and symbols and so are not colonial or exploitative. Rather they carry on the oral tradition at many levels, furthering and nourishing it and being furthered and nourished by it" (*Sacred* 79). Simon Ortiz sees no necessary conflict in the employment of Western literary forms. For him contemporary mediational texts may express both traditional goals and a new literary tradition. He writes, "of the creative ability of Indian people to gather in many forms of the socio-political colonizing force which beset them and to make these forms meaningful in their own terms. . . . They [Western forms] are now Indian because of the creative development that the native people applied to them" ("Toward" 8).[2] Both of these writers speak eloquently of the potential of their mediative positioning.

Allen and Ortiz choose to emphasize the ultimate Native goals of their own writings and that done by their contemporaries. Looking at the same body of work, Arnold Krupat sees the mediational mix as "influenced in a very substantial degree by the central forms of Western, or first world literature." He renames what I refer to as contemporary Native American Literature as "indigenous literature." For Krupat the work of Silko, Momaday and others, "manages successfully to merge forms internal to his [the Native writer] cultural formation with forms external to it, but pressing upon, even seeking to delegitimate it" (*Voice* 214). What each critic sees but from a different perspective is the same as what each reader perceives—the constantly changing texture of mediation, the possibilities of realigning and reinforcing the reader's epistemology. The successful contemporary Native

---

[2] Ortiz argues that against those who would see contemporary writers as not writing authentic "Indian" literature. For him, the cultural goal overcomes any delegitimating influence of the form used: "The ways and methods have been important, but they are important only because of the reason for the struggle. And it is that reason—the struggle against colonialism—which has given substance to what is authentic" ("Toward" 9). As he continues to argue that this struggle engenders a nationalistic quality in contemporary Native American Literature, he concludes: "This is the crucial item that has to be understood, that it is entirely possible for a people to retain and maintain their lives through the use of any language. There is not a question of authenticity here; rather it is the way that Indian people have creatively responded to forced colonization" ("Toward" 10). While he tends to see the contemporary Native writer's goal in political terms, I think he would agree that the realization of the political goal necessitates a restructured cognitive framework for the implied non-Native reader. Such a shift may also be necessary for the implied Native reader who is expected to accept as a cultural tool what was previously seen as a colonial imposition.

writer can create a text which merges delegitimizing influences while continuing oral tradition and culture. The text is substantially Native and substantially Western. In seeking its complex goals, it must adopt and transfer each culture's means of knowledge and value formation. This back and forth, the assertion and reassertion of value and form creates multi-dimensional understanding for each reader. The best work of Momaday, Silko, Welch, Vizenor, Allen, and many others mediates as it illuminates, juxtaposing cultural traditions on conscious and unconscious levels.

Yet these writers know that a writer can not guarantee the reactions of real readers. Consequently the texts they generate assign roles for Native and non-Native readers to assume. The concept of the implied reader as outlined by Wayne Booth is useful here to remind us that writers expect readers to respond in certain ways, such as laugh, be curious or be afraid, even if they know they can not completely manipulate them. Iser elaborates on this insight with his discussions on textual perspectives, finding the role of the implied reader inherent in the text. Gerard Genette further specifies that the implied reader, often consisting "wholly of the signs that imply and sometimes designate him" can be deduced "by the competence—linguistic and narrative, among other kinds—that the text postulates in expecting to be read" (148-49).[3] Contemporary Native American writers construct implied readers through the textual perspective presupposed and through the narrative competence required, but also, because they are moving from one worldview to another, implied readers require certain epistemological competence at various points in the text. The writers hope that the readers will assume these roles. To secure as much of a fusion between real and implied readers as possible, it is often the case that integrated meaning can only be achieved when the fusion is complete.

As the writer strives to bring the oral into the written, the Native American vision into Western thinking, spirit into modern identity, community into society, and myth into modern imagination, he or she is not confined to one cultural framework. While Native American writers do create devastating critiques of European American society, they express wider and deeper concerns than social criticism or a self-congratulatory view that all the old traditions, the old ways of perceiving are immutable and omnipotent. Contemporary Native American writ-

---

[3] Genette prefers the term "potential reader." I adopt implied reader because of the wide acceptance of the term.

ers insist on their freedom to use the tools and expectations of both Native and Western cultural codes to achieve the goals of the other as well as to satisfy the epistemological expectations of both audiences. N. Scott Momaday in *House Made of Dawn*, for instance, feels free to use both Native ceremonial ritual and modern literary stream of consciousness to set the implied reader's perceptual basis for mythic and sociological identity. As a participant in two literary and cultural traditions—Western and Native, the contemporary Native American writer is free to use the epistemological structures of one to penetrate the other, to stay within one cultural framework or to change twice on the same page. While terms like "Western" and "Native" establish large generalizations which could be considered to undermine cultural diversity in each arena, such generalizations serve to point the student of contemporary Native American Literature in useful directions. By "Western," I refer to those cultural backgrounds in common with the various groups of Europe and America. By "Native," I refer to the specific Native American cultural traditions with which the Native writer identifies, and any areas of commonality between the many other cultural traditions.

In an essay on Acoma poet Simon Ortiz, Kenneth Lincoln sees this utilization of two cultures in terms of past and present, "... being Indian involves not just the traditions or catastrophes served up on a buffalo chip of history, but a conscious set of choices. The central issue is what to fuse of the new and the old, improvisations and continuances from the past" ("Common" 83). For Native American writers, mediation is expressed through their artistic choices and is vital to the continuance of identity.

By reminding us of the chronological dimension of the alternating use of worldviews and ways of knowing in mediational texts, Lincoln draws our attention to the way in which the mediative text is embedded in the context of all other discourses which have occurred in Western and Native traditions, discourses at once, artistic, historical, and cultural. As discourse, the text is connected to other discourse through what James Clifford refers to as "the intersubjectivity of all speech" (41) and what Todorov interpreting Bakhtin calls "intertextuality" (*Bakhtin* 60). Clifford, Todorov, and Bakhtin, each in their own way call attention to how every discourse enters into relation with past discourses and expected future discourses, thereby vastly expanding a definition of the word "discourse" such as the one given by Julia Kristeva as "any enunciation that integrates in its structure the locutor and the listener, with the desire of the former to influence the latter" (1). Bakhtin asserts that "the dialogic orientation is obviously a characteristic phenomenon of all discourse. It is the natural aim of all living discourse. Discourse comes upon the discourse of the other on all the roads that lead to its object, and it cannot but enter into intense and lively interaction with it" (Todorov, *Bakhtin* 62). Contemporary Native American writers may evoke a number of discourse fields from Western and Native traditions. Mediation, then, doubles the contexts and spheres of discourse since it moves from one cultural tradition to another as well as connecting the locutor to the listener. One of the major paths toward the creation of a mediative text is through fusing and realigning the cultural patterns of discourse into the many elements of the text. The writer's sources run both chronologically through one sphere and cross-culturally between fields of discourse. In choosing "what to fuse of the old and the new," the writer decides how to engage previous discourse so that he or she will further its development and yet reveal how that sphere of discourse might find new ways of creating meaning, new ways of talking about what is meaningful inside its own field and other fields. In *Love Medicine*, Louise Erdrich uses oral tradition through oral history and symbolic, almost mythic events current with the lives of her characters to engage the on-going personal discourse of particular families while embedding it in larger and older fields of discourse. While implied non-Native readers recognize the form, they are led to question the assumptions about spiritual and communal meaning which underlie the discourse as implied Native readers must reevaluate the efficacy of such divergent discourse in creating continuing identity. The dynamic of mediation is similar to Michael Holquist's definition of Bakhtin's dialogism as a condition in which "Everything means, is understood, as a part of a greater whole—there is a constant interaction between meanings, all of which have the potential of conditioning others" (Bakhtin 426).

The necessity of mediation reaching out of a cultural framework to achieve its goals forces an element of self-reflexiveness into the text. The writer is prompted to consider the logic of presentation of cultural values, the questions of worldview, and presence of differing audiences as the text creates an ideological position in larger cultural conversations. Donald Bialostosky sees this self-reflexiveness in dialogic conversation because:

> Those who take turns speaking and listening, representing others and being represented by them, learn not just who these others are but who they themselves may be, not just what others may mean but what they themselves may mean among others. Whether the purview of such a conversation is a discipline, a culture, or a world of diverse cultures (and boundaries among these purviews are not

fixed and given in any case), the dialogic participants will both make it what it is and be made by it, conferring identities on their fellows and their communities, even as they receive identities from them. (792)

In the case of contemporary Native American Literature, the purview is both cultural and transcultural. Accordingly the cultural conversations engaged allow writers not only the chance to participate in a number of conversations, but also to see what they mean among others both inside their cultural conversations and across unfixed boundaries. They encourage implied readers to enter into conversations with which they are familiar and those with which they are not. However, no one ever has the last word. Each textual utterance awaits response and reinterpretation.

Consequently the mediative enterprise strives to be as self-critical of its perception and form as it is critical of other perceptions and forms. The act of mediation throws into doubt all epistemological laws even those governing its own formation, at least temporarily. Since mediation is as much about how we know and make meaning as it is about the social and cultural subjects delineated, it must tend toward metadiscursive reflexiveness as it weaves the locutor and the listener into that inclusive cultural web. In his discussion of discourse, Hayden White describes how discourse is always as much about interpretation as it is about the subject:

> A discourse moves 'to and fro' between received encodations of experience and the clutter of phenomena which refuses incorporation into conventional notions of "reality," "truth," or "possibility." It also moves "back and forth" (like a shuttle) between alternative ways of encoding this reality, some of which may be provided by the traditions of discourse prevailing in a given domain of inquiry and others of which may be idiolects of the author, the authority of which he is seeking to establish. Discourse, in a word, is quintessentially a *mediative* enterprise. As such, it is both interpretive and preinterpretive; it is always as much *about* the nature of interpretation itself as it is *about* the subject matter which is the manifest occasion of its own elaboration. (4)

As the mediative text moves back and forth between "ways of encoding this reality," implied readers reevaluate interpretation, are informed, and can be changed as they try on alternate epistemologies, different cultural goals, and different notions of reality and truth. While readers attempt to encode those phenomena which resist incorporation into their predisposed beliefs, the Native American writer offers reconstructed ways of encoding experience based on traditional and contemporary insight into both cultures. The mediational text moves the readers implied by the text to question the way they form knowledge and meaning, but in the end it seeks to reeducate those readers so that they can understand two codes, two traditions of discourse. Briefly, texts aspire to change readers. The more complete the fusion between the implied reader and the real reader, the more complete the change. Yet neither the writer nor the readers can completely escape the metadiscursive reflexiveness of the text which at one moment and for one reader highlights an element of one cultural code while simultaneously backgrounding it for another reader with a different cultural tradition.

It might be fruitful here to point out that this metadiscursive reflexiveness has been a prominent feature of postmodern American literature, at least, since the prominence of the writers of fabulation and metafiction of the seventies. This fact, of course, has not escaped the notice of contemporary Native American writers. Equally well known to Native writers is the phenomenon which Dennis Tedlock has presented to non-Natives that storytelling in the oral tradition establishes a dialectical relationship between "text and interpretation" (236). The interpretative and self-reflexive mode of oral discourse pervades the text, texture, and context of an oral event. This aspect of storytelling unites it with postmodern American literature. On this intermediate common ground, Native American oral tradition and contemporary American literature can meet. With this in mind, Allen's contention that contemporary Native writing can both nourish oral tradition and be nourished by it gains support.

As implied readers move from one worldview to another, from one field of discourse to another, back and forth through the chronological depth of those fields and back and forth between text and interpretation, they are brought to adopt a perspective on the meaning of the text, but this perspective is constantly changing, constantly being modified by a completely different set of epistemological codes. They can not help but ask themselves if their understanding of previous moments in the reading of the text was correct. Wolfgang Iser has discussed the manner in which a reader moves through a text, a manner which becomes central to the success of a mediational text: "Thus the reader's communication with the text is a dynamic process of self-correction, as he formulates signifieds which he must continually modify" (67). This formation and reformation of signifieds Iser has called misreading. As we read and then suspect we have misread, our perspective on all that has come before in the text changes. Through the process of reading the text, readers become something, someone they were not before. But more than that, if readers are open to the successful mediational text, they will tend to question their set of culturally determined assumptions about narrative, meaning, and life. Wallace Martin in his discussion of Iser's theories concludes:

> When a perspective on life proves inadequate, the reader tends to question the entire repertoire of conventional assumptions on which it is based. In Iser's view, narration progresses as a negation of partial and inadequate ways of understanding the world, leaving in its wake not a constructed meaning but a variety of hypothetical viewpoints depending on how the reader has filled in meanings, questioned social practices, and tried to find positive alternatives to the inadequate views represented in the text. If open to the experience the text provides, we are likely to find negations of some of our own views; as a result, the self that begins reading a book may not be quite the same self as the one that finishes it. (162)

Readers who finish a mediational text by a contemporary Native American writer will have been encouraged to examine not only their perspectives, but also their epistemology as they move back and forth in Native cultural conversations, and back and forth between Native and non-Native cultural codes. The end result is that they are now open to a Native epistemological pattern that they previously did not know how to see and to the new hybrid forms of meaning and knowledge that contemporary Native American writers can create. In the ending of *Wind from an Enemy Sky*, D'Arcy McNickle presents readers with an unexpected tragedy which arises from the good motives of both whites and Indians. The tragedy continues a historical conflict and is prophesied by a spiritual leader's vision. However, it makes no sense in traditional narrative expectations and comes as a shock. Readers struggle to find the meaning in it; they question why they didn't believe it was coming, even though it had been foreshadowed. They start to rethink what they have seen as meaningful events and logical behavior. They contemplate how they can act to avoid such tragedy. In the readers' conclusions rest the fruits of mediation.

Contemporary fiction seems ideally suited to achieve this epistemological restructuring.[4] Elaine Jahner argues that for the traditional storytellers, narratives were valued more as explorations of particular ways of knowing and learning than as static constructs of knowledge. Contemporary Native American storytellers of-

---

[4] Paula Allen sees much common narrative ground in contemporary fiction. In "American Indian Fiction," she writes, "For while ritual literature, either of the old-time, traditional variety or the new literary kind, is accretive rather than associative, achronistic rather than synchronistic, and ritual rather than mythological or historical, the new fiction of Europe and America provided a close enough analog to tribal literatures for writers to begin developing a new tribal literary tradition" (1058).

ten choose novels because "The novel is a narrative genre well-suited for examining how the traditional ways of knowing function in a multi-cultural world where the meanings of narrative are often twisted and tangled" ("Act" 45). The size and scope of the novel allows it the flexibility to juxtapose various narrative forms and then bring implied readers to a standpoint where they can untangle their responses and misreadings, following them back to their experiential roots. Since implied readers exist in a condition which is both self-reflexive and creative, real readers are more open to face the Other and themselves in the Other; they read and form hypotheses about meaning only to have those revised and their methods questioned. Mikhail Bakhtin refers to this process as "ideological translation":

> In a word, the novelistic plot serves to represent speaking persons and their ideological worlds. What is realized in the novel is the process of coming to know one's own language as it is perceived in someone else's system. There takes place within the novel an ideological translation of another's language, and an overcoming of its otherness—an otherness that is only contingent, external, illusory. (365)

The process which Bakhtin describes for the novel equally describes mediational texts. Mediation produces a text where various languages contend and are mutually translated. By language, Bakhtin means a sphere of discourse with a dynamic chronological dimension which defines an identity and ideological position. As the reader's language is translated, his conception of himself and his cultural code become translated. He sees his conceptions of Native and Western discourse and identity through someone else's system. The implied Native reader sees through the non-Native; the implied non-Native reader sees through the Native. An implied reader of a mediational text must conclude by the end of a text that his understanding is complete and adequate even though it has been challenged and is now altered. In that sense, the otherness has been illusory. The mediational world of the text may supply a place to assimilate the Other where the physical world may not. However it is not a world divorced from the political realities of contemporary Native American experience. As Bakhtin writes "a dialogue of languages is a dialogue of social forces" (365). A mediational text attempts to maneuver readers into taking a series of regenerated socio-political positions. An ideological translation takes place, though not a physical transmutation. However, real readers may be ready to act because they perceive things differently.

What generates this mediation of the text is not only the Native writer's bicultural heritage but also the existence of multiple audiences. Native American writers write for two audiences—non-Native and Native American—or in many cases three audiences—a local one, a pan-tribal one and a non-Native contemporary American one. The attempt to satisfy those audiences generates the peculiar construct of their art. Contemporary Native writers want more than merely to stand between two cultures satisfying one audience's expectations first, then the other's. Such discourse would not develop much unity. And, such a creative stance would only tend to reinforce each cultural code rather than be mutually illuminative. To illuminate and mediate, they utilize the different cultural codes simultaneously for then surprise and meaning will be created in the implied reader, overcoming the momentary and illusory confusion of meeting the Other. Such a position is the most viable one for a Native American writer who wishes to avoid the invitation to schizophrenia inherent in participating in two opposing cultural traditions.

However, such a position also presents unparalleled potential for interpretation and synthesis. Paula Gunn Allen theorizes that contemporary American Indians are always faced with a "dual perception of the world." Because Native writers feel compelled to explore how contemporary Native experience creates comprehensible patterns of life, they create a generative artistic discourse "that will not only reflect the dual perceptions of Indian/non-Indian but will reconcile them. The ideal metaphor will harmonize the contradictions and balance them so that internal equilibrium can be achieved, so that each perspective is meaningful, and in their joining psychic unity rather than fragmentation occurs" (*Sacred* 161). For Allen, the successful mediation harmonizes the contradictions, creating unity and legitimating both spheres of discourse.

Too much criticism of contemporary Native American writing has applied the epistemological expectations of only one cultural code—the non-Native one, ignoring the harmonizing and unifying of dual perspectives. In a provocative call for an "ethnocriticism," Arnold Krupat has adopted a critical stance which attempts "To alter or ambiguate Western narrative and explanatory categories . . . To practice ethnocriticism, at any rate, will require real engagement with the epistemological and explanatory categories of Others, most particularly as these animate and propel other narratives. The necessary sorts of movement, therefore are not only those between dominant Western paradigms but also those between Western paradigms and the as-yet-to-be-named paradigms of the Rest" (*Ethnocriticism* 113).

The limited scholarship Krupat wishes to replace uses accepted Western categories and methods of analysis. If this criticism has an anthropological orientation, it asks questions which essentially boil down to: How Native American is it, but only within accepted preconceptions. Is it consistent with the published literature we have on a certain tribe or with the critic's experience with individual members of a tribal group? If it has a sociological orientation, it asks questions concerned with the way Native American society has decayed or how the work criticizes American society and its values. If it has a psychological orientation, it may probe the nature of psychological motivation of character. Or it may adopt what is believed to be a Native perspective as it searches for the key referent in traditional culture such as a specific ritual or oral narrative, which the critic sees as representing the complexity of the text. All of these approaches reinforce the established paths of Western knowledge, or a limited notion of Native perspectives. Community, continuity, myth, ritual, and identity can easily be overlooked as the goals of the dominant discourse take over. Reed Way Dasenbrock has observed that "The temptations in studying such bicultural writers are to deny their biculturality, to privilege one of their formative cultures in the name of authenticity or the other in the name of universality. And the temptation is stronger when the cultures are so obviously not fused but still separate and in a state of tension and interaction" (317). The mediational text uses, at least, two perspectives so that neither is subsumed, but rather they exist in a dynamic confluence that encourages deeper cross-cultural questions in various audiences. An appropriate methodology to study such texts must also use, at least, two perspectives. A mediational approach might follow the formation of mythic patterns in the story while defining psychic unity or examine ritual meaning developed in a social confrontation.

Leslie Silko's novel *Ceremony* is an example of a richly mediated text. Silko's protagonist, Tayo, grows to an understanding of racism, American education, even nuclear power, as he begins to perceive the world in terms of the struggle in a medicineman's mythic story. Laguna storytelling discourse is juxtaposed to psychological determinations of meaning, and the non-Native world becomes illuminated through Laguna cultural understandings. Conversely, when Silko has Tayo realize that the path back to harmony with the land and Laguna culture requires that Tayo live again in the multiple present moment and that he must rely on the Laguna language, whose grammar subtly implies a world where the past and future exist linguistically always in the present, she voices a perception that posits an analysis of time and linguistic distinctions not arising out of traditional Laguna culture. Indeed, fundamental to an appreciation of the novel is the idea that the old ceremonies need to change. Tayo's survival and thus Laguna's will rely on the visions of people like an unorthodox Navajo medicineman and the mixed-blood marginalized Tayo. These elements propose epistemological lessons that the implied Native reader must learn. Ultimately Silko intimates that non-Native structures like the novel will help to create new ceremonies when the old kiva ceremonies have lost their efficacy. Some elements of Laguna epistemology are being challenged, while others are being reinforced at the same time as the non-Native audience is being challenged and satisfied. Familiar methods may be used to reach alien goals or vice versa. Silko's *Ceremony* skillfully mediates this new continent of old pathways.

Gerald Vizenor is another excellent writer who uses the potential of mediation to its fullest. In *Darkness in St. Louis Bearheart*, Vizenor presents a novel of a futuristic dystopia where gasoline is scarce. In it, he completely mythologizes the characters, their actions, and the purpose of the book. Actions are linked less with causation than with continuance on a mythic plane so that events resonate into significance on a number of epistemological planes, both Native and non-Native. On the other hand, Vizenor develops a psychological dimension of essentially mythic characters, though it is only to subvert his readers' expectations. Stylistically, he pursues narrative strategies similar to other contemporary avant-garde writers in order to present a satirical critique of American society and Native American survival. In other writings, Vizenor achieves a non-Native sociological goal such as when he analyzes the power structure of a university department through characters at once mythic and realistic. Vizenor's updated trickster tales place Native American perceptions in a modern framework to delight Native audiences. However, for non-Native audiences, he explains "I would like to imagine tribal experience for the non-Indian, whose frame of reference is very different from ours" (*Song* 165).

Allen emphasizes that this mediational artistic world is one very close to the actual lived experience of contemporary Native Americans, somewhere intertwined with two cultures and perspectives. In mediating through these differing perspectives, writers try to create patterns which harmonize. They draw on their mediational experience and dual perception of the world to create a mediational discourse. Hayden White outlines the relationship between discourse and experience when he writes, " . . . a discourse is itself a kind of model of the processes of consciousness by which a given area of experience, originally apprehended as simply a field of phenomena demanding understanding, is assimilated by analogy to those areas of experience felt to be *already* understood as to *their* essential natures" (4-5). The mediational experience of the Native American writer is passed on to implied readers as they struggle to bring meaning and psychic unity to the text.

Vizenor has written about mixed-bloods or metis as individuals with great creative potential. He calls them "earthdivers" (characters from tribal creation stories) who bring up small kernels of meaningful cultural sand, blowing on them with their trickster-inspired breath to create new turtle worlds of discourse. He sees this situation as similar to the position of contemporary Native writers. Ultimately for Vizenor, all Native Americans are metis and all non-Native are called to follow them:

> Metis earthdivers waver and forbear extinction in two worlds. Metis are the force in the earthdiver metaphor, the tension in the blood and the uncertain word, the imaginative and compassionate trickster on street corners in the cities. When the mixedblood earthdiver summons the white world to dive like the otter and beaver and muskrat in search of earth, and federal funds, he is both animal and trickster, both white and tribal, the uncertain creator in an urban metaphor based on a creation myth that preceded him in two world views and oral traditions. (*Earthdivers* xvii)

Whether by blood or experience, Native Americans today, but especially writers, express a mixed heritage. As the creation of new worlds from the old isolated worldviews proceeds, the writer acts out his or her role as mediator-creator. The existence of non-Native and Native audiences forces the contemporary Native American writer to evaluate consciously the cultural codes incorporated into the text as well as to evaluate which implied readers are paying attention to which elements in the text. In her interviews, Silko has commented on her need to weigh each element of the story to decide first which stories can be told effectively, and then how much to tell and in what detail. She does not want to lose an outsider by including too much Laguna detail, nor a Native American reader by overemphasizing goals and methods too Western. She consciously analyzes which cultural codes to use and to whom she is speaking at any one point in the text. Owens sees in this balancing as a "matrix of incredible heteroglossia and linguistic torsions and an intensely political situation" (*Other* 15).[5] This level of self-reflexiveness can also be seen as generating what Bakhtin would call "two-voiced discourse." Todorov interpreting Bakhtin contributes his gloss:

---

[5] Owens, following a similar line of reasoning, intelligently discusses contemporary Native literary texts as hybridized dialogue. Recognizing the Native and non-Native reader implied by the text, he explores heteroglossia and the political situation inherent in the texts (*Other* 11-16).

Two-voiced discourse is characterized by the fact that not only is it represented but it also refers simultaneously to two contexts of enunciation: that of the present enunciation and that of a previous one. Here the author "can also use the discourse of the other toward his own ends, in such a way that he imprints on this discourse, that already has, and keeps, its own orientation, a new semantic orientation. Such a discourse must, in principle, be perceived as being another's. A single discourse winds up having two semantic orientations, two voices." (*Bakhtin* 71).

Mediation is two-voiced discourse which appropriates one audience's discourse to force its own cognitive reorientation but it does so in two separate fields of discourse. The ultimate task of the contemporary Native American writer is to find ways to speak to multiple audiences at the same time and at different levels.[6]

Much contemporary anthropological theory has been engaged in a task similar to that of the contemporary Native American writer. There is a movement which concerns itself with how to turn the dominant anthropological discourse into a dialogue with the other. Clifford, Marcus, Fischer and others have spearheaded this inquiry which has attempted to clarify the lines of cross-cultural interaction. The literary scholar may find it useful to conceive of the world of mediational discourse as akin to Roy Wagner's concept of culture as an invented realm which the anthropologist creates to mediate between the reality of their world and ours. But more to the point, this mediational and cultural world incorporates the discourse of the Other, but from both conceptions of the Other, both audiences' perceptions. It seems to me that Native American writers successfully complete the task that contemporary anthropology sets out for itself when along with the ideal anthropological dialogue, it "creates a world, or an understanding of the *differences between* two worlds, that exists between persons who were indeterminately far apart, in all sorts of ways, when they started out on their conversation" (Tedlock 323), but they have now conversed in a new grammar.

---

6 Andrew Wiget explores this "multivocality of some narrative, when the voice of the present narration ... is located in and made intelligible by its relationship with another, earlier voice also represented in the narration." His analysis seeks to define artistic authority as an effect of this multivocality. However, rather than a dialogic interaction, he interprets identity, voice, and authority as rhetorical constructions "as well as ethnographic reality" ("Identity" 258).

WORKS CITED

Allen, Paula Gunn. "American Indian Fiction, 1968-1983." *A Literary History of the American West*. Fort Worth: Texas Christian UP, 1987.

———. *The Sacred Hoop: Recovering the Feminine in American Indian Traditions*. Boston: Beacon P, 1986.

Bakhtin, M. M. *The Dialogic Imagination: Four Essays by M. M. Bakhtin*. Ed. Michael Holquist. Trans. Caryl Emerson and Michael Holquist. Austin and London: U of Texas P, 1981.

Clifford, James. *The Predicament of Culture: Twentieth-Century Ethnography, Literature, and Art*. Cambridge: Harvard UP, 1988.

Dasenbrock, Reed Way. "Forms of Biculturalism in Southwestern Literature: The Work of Rudolfo Anaya and Leslie Marmon Silko." *Genre* XXI (Fall 1988): 307-20.

Erdrich, Louise. *Love Medicine*. New York: Holt, 1984.

———. "Where I Ought to Be: A Writer's Sense of Place," *New York Times Book Review*, 90 (28 July 1985): 1, 23-24.

Genette, Gerard. *Narrative Discourse Revisited*. Trans. Jane E. Lewin. 1983. Ithaca: Cornell UP, 1988.

Iser, Wolfgang. *The Act of Reading*. Baltimore and London: Johns Hopkins UP, 1978.

Jahner, Elaine. "An Act of Attention: Event Structure in *Ceremony*." *American Indian Quarterly* 5.1 (1979): 37-46.

Kristeva, Julia. *Language the Unknown: an Initiation into Linguistics*. New York: Columbia UP, 1989.

Krupat, Arnold. *The Voice in the Margin: Native American Literature and the Canon*. Berkeley: U of California P, 1989.

———. *Ethnocriticism: Ethnography, History, Literature*. Berkeley: U of California P, 1992.

Lincoln, Kenneth. "Common Walls: The Poetry of Simon Ortiz." *Coyote Was Here: Essays on Contemporary Native American Literary and Political Mobilization*. Ed. Bo Scholer. Aarhus, Denmark: Seklos, 1984.

McNickle, D'Arcy. *Wind from an Enemy Sky*. Albuquerque: U of New Mexico P, 1978.

Marcus, G. E. and Michael Fischer. *Anthropology as Cultural Critique: an Experimental Moment in the Human Services*. Chicago: U of Chicago P, 1986.

Martin, Wallace. *Recent Theories of Narrative*. Ithaca: Cornell UP, 1986.

Momaday, N. Scott. *House Made of Dawn*. New York: Harper, 1968.

Ortiz, Simon. "Toward a National Indian Literature: Cultural Authenticity in Nationalism," *MELUS* 8.2 (Summer 1981): 7-12.

Owens, Louis. *Other Destinies: Understanding the American Indian Novel*. Norman: U of Oklahoma P, 1992.

Silko, Leslie. *Ceremony*. New York: Viking, 1977.

Tedlock, Dennis. *The Spoken Word and the Work of Interpretation*. Philadelphia: U of Pennsylvania P, 1983.

Todorov, Tzvetan. *Mikhail Bakhtin: The Dialogical Principle*. Trans. Wlad Godzich. Minneapolis: U of Minnesota P, 1984.

Vizenor, Gerald. *Darkness in Saint Louis Bearheart*. 1978. Retitled *Bearheart: The Heirship Chronicles*. Minneapolis: U of Minnesota P, 1990.

___. *Earthdivers: Tribal Narratives on Mixed Descent*. Minneapolis: U of Minnesota P, 1981.

___. "Gerald Vizenor." *This Song Remembers: Self-Portraits of Native Americans in the Arts*. Ed. Jane Katz. Boston: Houghton Mifflin, 1980.

___. "Introduction." *Narrative Chance: Postmodern Discourse on Native American Indian Literatures*. Ed. Gerald Vizenor. Albuquerque: U of New Mexico P, 1989.

White, Hayden. *Tropics of Discourse: Essays in Cultural Criticism*. Baltimore and London: Johns Hopkins UP, 1978.

Wiget, Andrew. "Identity, Voice, and Authority: Artist-Audience Relations in Native American Literature," *World Literature Today* 66:2 (1992): 258-63.

Andrew Blackbird's Smallpox Story
Helen Jaskoski, California State University, Fullerton

Written literature by North American Indian authors consisted, until the present century, almost entirely of nonfiction prose. Polemical and historical writings, often directed to an ignorant, indifferent or hostile non-Indian audience, generally had the dual aims of correcting erroneous or biased views of Indians and of preserving their national traditions. Writing of comparable Latin American texts, Mary Louise Pratt uses Francoise Lionnet's term "autoethnography" to designate a genre of

> texts in which people undertake to describe themselves in ways that engage with representations others have made of them....[these texts] involve a selective collaboration with and appropriation of idioms of the metropolis or the conqueror. These are merged or infiltrated to varying degrees with indigenous idioms to create self-representations intended to intervene in metropolitan modes of understanding. Autoethnographic works are often addressed to both metropolitan audiences and the speaker's own community. Their reception is thus highly indeterminate. (35)

Among the most interesting of the North American autoethnographies are some half-dozen histories of the colonial and postcolonial Great Lakes area, written by nineteenth-century woodlands authors from both sides of the U.S./Canadian border. LaVonne Ruoff's bibliography notes histories written by Peter Jones and George Copway (Canadian Ojibwa), Peter Dooyentate Clarke (Wyandot), David Cusick and Chief Elias Johnson (Tuscarora), William Warren (Minnesota Ojibwa) and the Ottawa chief Andrew J. Blackbird (63-64). Interesting in themselves as examples of a rhetoric mediating between diverse audiences, these texts also offer an opportunity to reassess the prevailing history of the period and interrogate notions such as "culture contact" and "frontier" (a critical project recently called for by Annette Kolodny). This paper offers a contribution to that process by examining a particular element of the historical tradition—smallpox stories. I focus on Andrew Blackbird's *History of the Ottawa and Chippewa Indians of Michigan* because Blackbird's story is of unusual interest both narratively and historically.

During the long process of European conquest and colonization, contagious disease destroyed the western hemisphere's first nations on a scale that far outweighed military conquest. Of all these plagues, smallpox was the most devastating; according to one historian of the subject, "war, famine and all other causes of death combined could not be compared to smallpox" (Sheehan 229). The written history of these epidemics has derived almost entirely from colonial documents.[1] However, the indigenous peoples of the Americas also maintained records of smallpox epidemics, preserved in their oral traditions.

The most widely known smallpox story is not by an Indian, but appears in the sixth edition of Francis Parkman's *The Conspiracy of Pontiac* (1871). Parkman reviews the 1763 correspondence between Sir Jeffrey Amherst, commander of British forces in North America, and Colonel Henry Bouquet in western Pennsylvania, in which the officers plan to distribute infected blankets to the Indians around Fort Pitt. The story appalled Parkman, who was unable to ascertain whether the plan had actually been carried out (subsequent research indicated that it had; see Knollenberg).

A similar story, written down by William Warren, an Ojibwa politician and scholar, appears in his *History of the Ojibway People* (written 1850; published posthumously 1885). Warren writes about an epidemic in the 1780s among the Pillager band of Ojibwas living north and west of Lake Superior; the infection was believed to have come to the Pillagers in an infected bundle of textiles given them by the commander of Fort Mackinac. Like Parkman, Warren was hesitant to believe that British officers would undertake biological warfare; he searched out another explanation and found an alternative story. In this second account, the infection originated with the taking of scalps by a war party and was passed from village to village by returning warriors and the people they had contact with. If William Warren had been able to see the documents that Francis Parkman reviewed, he might have given more credence to the story of infected trade goods. In any case, both authors invoke the theme of smallpox as culture contact by way of disease, and both are

---

[1] The best summary of these records, most of them still archival, is Stearn and Stearn.

susceptible to the suspicion, ambivalence, denial, and uncertainty expressed in the stories they record. The nature of history and the relationship between narrative imagination and historical fact become problematic in these stories, as they do in yet another one. A third smallpox story, related by Andrew J. Blackbird, has a unique focus and is interesting both for its narrative shaping and its possible relation to the historical record.

Andrew J. Blackbird was a member of a distinguished Ottawa family from the northwest shore of the Michigan lower peninsula. He wrote his *History of the Ottawa and Chippewa Indians of Michigan* (1887) late in life, after a long career in education, politics and public service. Blackbird's book, like many similar autoethnographic texts, is a combination of autobiography, history, ethnography and polemic. He opens with a conventional reference to inaccuracy in the prevailing view of Indians and announces his intention to set the record straight. In the course of correcting the record of an unnamed historian, Blackbird relates the story, preserved by elders of his nation, of a smallpox epidemic during the height of the French and Indian war, about 1757.[2] Andrew Blackbird's story is remarkable among oral histories of smallpox epidemics for the unusual nature of the disease vector. This record of an early epidemic in an oral history collected by an Indian historian provides an opportunity to examine the dynamic between the storyteller's shaping artistry and the historian's verifiability.

Blackbird introduces his story by asserting that, contrary to the "noted historian" criticized earlier, there were several notable chiefs among the Ottawas at the time of the destruction of Fort Michilimackinac in 1763, at the height of Pontiac's war; these leaders included his own father, grandfather and great-grandfather. Blackbird then goes on to explain that these men were survivors of a much larger population:

> However it was a notable fact that by this time [1763] the Ottawas were greatly reduced in numbers from what they were in former times, on account of the small-

---

[2] It seems as though the noted historian, to whom Blackbird adverts again, might have been Francis Parkman, whose series on the French and English in America was enormously successful. However, if Parkman's *The Conspiracy of Pontiac* was the history alluded to, Blackbird makes no mention of the famous story of the British officers' conspiracy to distribute infected blankets from the smallpox hospital at Fort Pitt during the summer of 1763. It is possible that Blackbird saw one of the earlier editions of *The Conspiracy of Pontiac;* according to Parkman's introduction to the sixth edition, published in 1870, discovery of the smallpox story was one of the main reasons he undertook a revision of the earlier text.

pox which they brought from Montreal during the French war with Great Britain. This smallpox was sold to them shut up in a tin box, with the strict injunction not to open the box on their way homeward, but only when they should reach their country; and that this box contained something that would do them great good, and their people! The foolish people believed really there was something in the box supernatural, that would do them great good. Accordingly, after they reached home they opened the box; but behold there was another tin box inside, smaller. They took it out and opened the second box, and behold, still there was another box inside of the second box, smaller yet. So they kept on this way till they came to a very small box, which was not more than an inch long; and when they opened the last one they found nothing but mouldy particles in this last little box! They wondered very much what it was, and a great many closely inspected to try to find out what it meant. But alas, alas! pretty soon burst out a terrible sickness among them. The great Indian doctors themselves were taken sick and died. The tradition says it was indeed awful and terrible. Every one taken with it was sure to die. Lodge after lodge was totally vacated—nothing but the dead bodies lying here and there in their lodges—entire families being swept off with the ravages of this terrible disease. The whole coast of Arbor Croche, . . . a continuous village some fifteen or sixteen miles long . . . was entirely depopulated and laid waste. It is generally believed among the Indians of Arbor Croche that this wholesale murder of the Ottawas by this terrible disease sent by the British people, was actuated through hatred, and expressly to kill off the Ottawas and Chippewas because they were friends of the French Government or French King. (9-10)

Along with the unique feature of the set of nested boxes we can recognize themes of invisibility, treachery and revenge that pervade other smallpox stories. The story's place and function within Blackbird's history, and its relationship to other sources of information about contemporary smallpox epidemics, show Blackbird to have been a careful historian as well as a subtle shaper of narrative and a dedicated polemicist.

The box of smallpox calls to mind instances of allegorical or symbolic smallpox vectors: the Kiowa story, for example, in which smallpox is a diseased man riding on the plains (Marriott), or the Wyandot tale in which smallpox is drunk from a bottle and later countered by skunk scent (Feer). However, both internal textual evidence and external contextual records suggest that Andrew Blackbird's box of smallpox is plausibly literal and actual, rather than metaphorical or allegorical.

Blackbird's placement of the smallpox story in the opening paragraphs of his text serves his dual purpose of not only correcting the factual record, but also bringing to light the moral record of injustice and mistreatment. The event recorded in the smallpox story parallels a later incident which Blackbird has described in the immediately preceding paragraphs. Before telling the smallpox story Blackbird relates the Ottawas' account of what happened at the famous massacre, in 1763, of the British occupants of Fort Michilimackinac:

> [T]here were several Ottawa chiefs living on the south side of the Straits at this particular time, who took no part in this massacre, but took by force the few survivors of this great, disastrous catastrophe, and protected them for a while and afterwards took them to Montreal, presenting them to the British Government. (7)

The reward for the Ottawas' efforts was the British government's promise of amity, protection—and liquor. The passage is worth quoting at some length for its exposition of Blackbird's method as historian and rhetorician and for comparison to his rhetoric in telling the smallpox story:

> According to our understanding in our traditions, that was the time the British Government made such extraordinary promises to the Ottawa tribe of Indians, at the same time thanking them for their humane action upon those British remnants of the massacre. She promised them that her long arms will perpetually extend around them from generation to generation, so long as there should be rolling sun. They should receive gifts from her sovereign in shape of goods, provisions, firearms, ammunition, and intoxicating liquors! Her sovereign's beneficent arm should be even extended unto the dogs belonging to the Ottawa tribe of Indians. And what place soever she should meet them, she would freely unfasten the faucet which contains her living water— whiskey, which she will also cause to run perpetually and freely unto the Ottawas as the fountain of perpetual spring! (8)

The account presents strong if implicit parallels with the smallpox story which is narrated next. In both cases delegations of Ottawas visit Montreal, bringing with them valuable exchange goods: after the massacre they transport British prisoners for reward, whereas earlier their cargo had probably been fur, which they would have traded for goods, including the fatal box. In both cases they receive in return extravagant promises, and in both cases a commodity which is proffered as having almost magically beneficent properties turns out to be an agent of horrible destruction. Trade becomes treachery; the secret of flowing fountain and magic box is invisible death and long-lasting deterioration.

The image that stands out in each story is the gift, the bountiful fountain paralleling the set of nested boxes. However, the rhetoric in the two passages contrasts in tone and in approach to the audience. A catalogue of British-provided "goods, provisions, firearms, ammunition, and intoxicating liquors" ends in an exclamation point, to be followed by the sarcastic reference to the "sovereign's beneficent arm .. even extended unto the dogs" of the Indians and then by the reference to the "faucet which contains her living water." Everything about the passage underscores its metaphoric, allusive, decidedly literary qualities. Hyperbole in the reference to dogs, metonymy and personification to describe the government and its sovereign's far-reaching arm, are enriched with Biblical echoes in fountain and spring.[3]

The box of smallpox described in the next few paragraphs might be another powerful figure of speech, recalling legends of hidden evil in caskets and Pandora's boxes. The description of the box, however, proceeds in a tone of factual understatement and journalistic reporting. There is one brief exclamatory statement— "nothing but mouldy particles!"—and the expression of grief at such a loss. But the passage lacks metaphor, irony, allusion or rhetorical ornamentation of any kind. The incident is reported as fact, not allegory.

The distinction is consistent with Blackbird's treatment of legend, myth and history throughout his book. For instance, in describing an earlier massacre of an Indian community on Mackinac Island, he carefully distinguishes the massacre story, which he considers to be historical, from a romantic legend that grew up around the two survivors. The latter story, he says, "may be considered, at this age, as a fictitious story; but every Ottawa and Chippewa to this day believes it to be positively so" (21). The chapter in which this episode is related begins with a headnote that reinforces the distinction Blackbird wants to make by referring twice to the "Earliest Possible Known History of Mackinac Island" and "Its Historical Definition" in contrast to "The Legends of the Two Who Escaped." Andrew Blackbird had long experience communicating by way of oratory and writing with a non-Indian audience, and he framed his written history to make it possible for that audience to accept his careful distinctions and scrutiny of legends, and thus be more

---

[3] Blackbird, a devout Protestant convert from Catholicism when he wrote his History, would have found several allusions in the Authorized (King James) Version of the New Testament, among them the Gospel of John 4.14 ("But whosoever drinketh of the water that I shall give him shall never thirst; but the water that I shall give him shall be in him a well of water springing up into everlasting life") and Revelation 7.17 ("For the Lamb which is in the midst of the throne shall feed them, and shall lead them unto living fountains of waters; and God shall wipe away all tears from their eyes"). Blackbird's implicit contrast of the ideals and classical texts of Christianity with the actual words and actions of the purveyors of that religion belongs to a long tradition of critique of institutionalized Christianity, including much abolitionist literature as well as writings by other nineteenth-century North American Indian authors.

likely to accept him as a reliable mediator and reporter of Ottawa history. Yet Blackbird's strategic address to his non-Indian audience embraces a contradiction: presenting himself as a reliable mediator who can perceive the important distinction between fictitious story and real history, his authority for that history rests in his identity as one of those Ottawa, every one of whom believes the "fictitious" account "to be positively so." This alienating aspect of the mediating role is an issue that every American Indian author has had to contend with.

Chapter 9 of the *History* appeals to another element in the non-Indian audience, his conservative Christian readers. In this chapter Blackbird presents two of the great myths of Ne-naw-bozhoo: the story of the flood and the earth-diver, and the legend of the hero swallowed by the water monster. In the course of introducing these founding myths to his non-Indian audience Blackbird points out parallels between these traditions and the Biblical stories of Noah and Jonah. In an age and to an audience which regarded native traditions as at best harmless superstition and at worst devil worship, Blackbird's claims are positive and unapologetic, yet undefensive: "These are some of the legends told among the Ottawa and Chippewa Indians, as related in their own language, which are in some things quite similar to the records of the Bible" (78). In another chapter he adopts an attitude more detached than most of his non-Indian contemporaries toward popular theories that Indians were descended from the "lost tribes" of Israel, remarking that "From [the] evidence of working in metals and from the many other relics of former occupants, it is evident that this country has been inhabited for many ages, but whether by descendants of the Jews or of other Eastern races there is no way for us to determine" (96). In this skepticism Andrew Blackbird was ahead of many respected scientists of his day. To secular readers today Blackbird's text presents careful and subtle distinctions between the allegorical, the mythical, the fanciful, on one hand, and on the other hand what is "positively so" as history, as fact. The smallpox story falls within the second category: Blackbird regarded this account as factual, and wrote in such a way as to persuade his readers of its factuality.

External evidence from the context of the events Blackbird wrote about also supports the hypothesis that the box of smallpox is not a fanciful legend—however apt—but was probably real. In the period Andrew Blackbird was writing about, the last fifty years of the eighteenth century, smallpox inoculation had gained widespread acceptance in England and was also practiced in France. We are familiar today with a smallpox vaccine originally developed by Edward Jenner in England; Jenner's vaccine derived from cowpox, a virus harmful to cattle but which produces in humans immunity to smallpox. However, until Jenner's method was adopted in the latter part of the eighteenth century, immunization against smallpox was accomplished through inoculation, a very different procedure from vaccination.

Smallpox inoculation involved deliberate infection of a subject with variola, the live smallpox virus, taken from an infected individual. The hoped-for outcome was a mild case of the disease which would result in permanent immunity. Inoculation was a risky procedure and was only successful under conditions of rigorous quarantine. The rates of death from inoculation-induced smallpox were estimated at one in fifty (compared to one in six when the disease was contracted fortuitously [Miller 117-123, 125]); however, among Indian populations the success rate tended to be lower (Duffy).

The practice of inoculation is dated to the eleventh century in China and was known in Africa and the middle east; translations of Chinese medical treatises were a major means of promoting smallpox inoculation in eighteenth-century Europe and the Americas.[4] The "mouldy particles" that Andrew Blackbird says caused an infection among the Ottawa Indians sound remarkably like the infectious matter introduced in the process of inoculation. Chinese medical textbooks offer descriptions of classic inoculation procedures. One such work, the *Golden Mirror of Medicine,* describes four methods of smallpox inoculation; two of them are as follows:

(1) "The nose is plugged with powdered smallpox scabs laid on cotton wool...(2)...The powdered scabs are put into the end of a silver tube which is about six or seven inches long and curved at the end. The scabs are blown into the nose" (Hume 140).

What methods were recommended for transporting the infected matter are not described in the sources I have seen, but a set of nested boxes would satisfy the practical and emotional need for avoiding accidental contamination.

Is it possible that a container of smallpox matter collected for the purpose of inoculation was available in Montreal, and that it came into the hands of a group

---

[4] Several accounts point out that African slaves taught European colonizers in the western hemisphere how to inoculate for smallpox. Catholic missionaries carried out inoculation campaigns among Indians in Latin America, which were moderately successful when they were accepted, though not as effective as among Europeans. British colonists evidently did not attempt to inoculate Indians to prevent smallpox. Later, with the introduction of Jenner's vaccination method, Jefferson promoted the first of a number of United States government campaigns to immunize Indian populations against smallpox (Duffy; Sheehan; Stearn and Stearn).

of Indians from Michigan, who carried the infection home and who then contracted a much more severe case of the disease than would have been expected among
European subjects? Jesuit missionaries in China were much involved in studying
and translating classical Chinese treatises of all kinds, and they were important
agents in introducing Chinese knowledge and culture into Europe; furthermore,
Jesuit missionaries had been active in carrying out inoculation campaigns among
indigenous peoples in Latin America. There was a Jesuit mission at L'Arbre Croche
(Henry 47). Individual links for such a connection exist, but it is precisely the nature of the frontier as an "abyss" between the two cultures undergoing "contact"
that precludes our ever being certain on this question. The answer to the source of
Andrew Blackbird's box has disappeared into that abyss.

One other issue arises with respect to Blackbird's rhetoric and historiography.
It seems, from other records, that his account actually conflates two different epidemics. The opening sentences of his story, which date the epidemic to the last
years of the French and Indian war, would allude to the great epidemic which
passed throughout New France from 1755-1757; this plague was so devastating
that not only were military campaigns aborted, but most trading operations along
the Great Lakes had to be abandoned (Duffy 336; Stearn and Stearn 43-44). This
is the epidemic that decimated the populations around Fort Mackinac and in the
islands of the straits connecting Lakes Michigan and Huron. However, the destruction of L'Arbre Croche, a fifteen-mile-long town on the northwestern shore of the
lower Michigan peninsula, which Blackbird mentions at the end of his story, took
place some fifty years later, around 1799, in a different pandemic that swept
through the former French territories from upper Canada as far south as Louisiana
(Stearn and Stearn 51- 52).[5] It appears that Blackbird has synthesized the two episodes into a single narrative.

This collapsing of temporal distinctions between events that are thematically
related but separate in time is characteristic of oral traditions. In the Preface to his
history of the western Ojibwa, William Warren notes it as a difficult issue for the
historian: "Through the somewhat uncertain manner in which the Indians count
time, the dates of events . . . may differ slightly from those . . . endorsed by present
standard historians as authentic" (26). This rhetorical strategy is related to the

---

[5] Tanner's map of smallpox and other epidemics shows a major smallpox epidemic in the islands of the straits in 1757-58 (as well as 1670-71 and 1681-82) and another in the Little Traverse region, where L'Arbre Croche was located, in 1800-01
(170).

character of Blackbird's *History* as autoethnography. Andrew Blackbird's agenda as a historian, to "intervene" in the official story of the frontier, is less served by documenting chronology than by conveying the disruption, corrosion, and pillage that characterized the frontier as the indigenous population experienced it. The introduction of smallpox into the Ottawa population is an origin story, the account of a paradigmatic event which was, unfortunately, re-enacted many times. Its character as paradigm, however, does not conflict with the possible existence of the objects described in it.

Glenn Farris notes that all too often Native American oral traditions are "patronized as 'legend' or some form of 'just-so' stories without basis in fact, when in reality they often form valid oral history" (471). Native American writers of history have also been dismissed, through neglect as well as condescension, yet when read carefully—as carefully as they wrote—they are a necessary as well as enriching part of the story of the continent.

WORKS CITED

Bible. Authorized (King James) Version. Philadelphia: National Bible P, 1963.

Blackbird, Andrew J. *History of the Ottawa and Chippewa Indians of Michigan.* Ypsilanti, MI: The Ypsilantian Job Printing House, 1887. Petoskey, MI: Little Traverse Regional Historical Society, 1977.

Duffy, John. "Smallpox and the Indians in the American Colonies." *Bulletin of the History of Medicine.* Vol. 25 Baltimore: Johns Hopkins UP, 1951.

Farris, Glenn J. "Recognizing Indian Folk History as Real History: A Fort Ross Example." *American Indian Quarterly* 13 (1989): 471-480.

Feer, Michael. "'The Skunk and the Smallpox': Mythology and Historical Reality." *Plains Anthropologist* 18 (1973): 33-39.

Henry, Alexander. *Travels and Adventures in Canada.* New York: I. Riley, 1809. March of America Facsimile Series Number 43. Ann Arbor: University Microfilms, 1966.

Hume, Edward H. *The Chinese Way in Medicine.* Westport, CN: Hyperion P, Inc., 1940.

Knollenberg, Bernhard. "General Amherst and Germ Warfare." *Mississippi Valley Historical Review* 41 (1954): 489-494.

Kolodny, Annette. "Letting Go Our Grand Obsessions: Notes Toward a New Literary History of the American Frontiers." *American Literature* 64.1 (1992): 1-18.

Lionnet, Françoise. "Autoethnography: The An-Archic Style of *Dust Tracks on a Road.*" In *Autobiographical Voices: Race, Gender, Self-Portraiture.* 1989. Rpt. in Andrews, Williams L. *African American Autobiography: A Collection of Critical Essays.* Englewood Cliffs, NJ: Prentice Hall, 1993. 113-137.

Marriott, Alice and Carol K. Rachlin. *American Indian Mythology.* New York: Thomas Y. Crowell, 1968.

Miller, Genevieve. *The Adoption of Inoculation for Smallpox in England and France.* Philadelphia: U of Pennsylvania P, 1957.

Parkman, Francis. *The Conspiracy of Pontiac and The Indian War after the Conquest of Canada.* 2 vols. 1870. Frontenac edition vols. 14 & 15. New York: Charles Scribner's Sons, 1915.

Pratt, Mary Louise. "Arts of the Contact Zone." *Profession 91.* New York: MLA, 1991. 35-39.

Ruoff, A. LaVonne Brown. *American Indian Literatures: An Introduction, Bibliographic Review, and Selected Bibliography.* New York: MLA, 1990.

Sheehan, Bernard. *Seeds of Extinction: Jeffersonian Philanthropy and the American Indian.* Chapel Hill: U of North Carolina P, 1973.

Stearn, E. Wagner and Allen E. Stearn. *The Effect of Smallpox on the Destiny of the Amerindian.* Boston: Bruce Humphries, 1945.

Tanner, Helen Hornbeck. *Atlas of Great Lakes Indian History.* Norman and London: U of Oklahoma P, 1987.

Warren, William W[hipple]. *History of the Ojibway People.* Minneapolis: Minnesota Historical Society, 1885. Rpt. with Intro. by W. Roger Buffalohead, 1984.

The New "Frontier" of Native American Literature: Dis-Arming History with Tribal Humor

Kimberly M. Blaeser, University of Wisconsin, Milwaukee

> History begins with the implausible conception of the evolution of the interpretation of other implausibles, designated as facts.
>
> Gordon Henry, *The Light People*

i
Whose History is This Anyway?

In his 1987 introduction to *Harper's Anthology of 20th Century Native American Poetry*, Brian Swann characterizes Native American poetry as "poetry of historic witness" which "grows out of a past that is very much a present" (xvii). In his 1985 forward to the anthology *New and Old Voices of Wah'kon-tah: Contemporary Native American Poetry*, Vine Deloria, Jr. claims native poetry will "tell you more about the Indian's travels in historical experience than all the books written and lectures given" (ix-x). These statements of Swann and Deloria point to an essential strand in the web of all contemporary Native American literature: the weight of history. I don't mean to claim simply that history *informs* native literature, but rather that in a very real way history *forms* native writing. It provides, of course, much of the subject and the impetus, but beyond that the consciousness of historical continuum is sounded in the voice of native writers, and traced in the form and methods of their literary expression. Much of contemporary Indian literature in style alone writes itself against the events of Indian/White contact and, perhaps more importantly, against the past accounting of those events.

Deloria characterizes the work of the native writers as presenting a "reflective statement of what it means and has meant to live in a present which is continually overwhelmed by the fantasies of others of the meanings of past events" (x). Indeed, any discussion of the literary representation of history in the Americas finds it center in the notion of possession, not merely physical possession of the land and its resources, but ideological possession, because to a large degree the two have gone hand in hand: those who control the land, have controlled the story (the his-story) of the land and its people. This possession of history has compelled not merely the "facts," but the perspective of the accounts and the methods of representation as well. In his introduction to the collection *American Indians and the Problem of History*, Calvin Martin, for example, discusses the standard imposition of an anthropological perspective onto the history of Native American people who themselves proceed from a biological metaphysic and he characterizes such a move as "ideological colonization" (9). The situation is further complicated because, of course, the creation and interpretations of histories have also functioned directly as the justifications for possession or dispossession, and the forums for supposed historical accounts have always included the various literary genres. Among the many contemporary scholars who have recognized these connections between history, literature and colonization are Richard Drinnon *(Facing West: The Metaphysics of Indian-Hating and Empire Building)*, Richard Slotkin *(Regeneration Through Violence: The Mythology of the American Frontier, 1600-1860)*, and Ward Churchill, whose recent study *Fantasies of the Master Race: Literature, Cinema and the Colonization of American Indians* includes subsections entitled "History as Propaganda of the Victors" and "Literature as a Weapon in the Colonization of the American Indian."

In the trenches of the Native American literary movement, the responses to the representations and misrepresentations of history have appeared in many forms ranging from Neihardt's rendering of Black Elk's account of Little Big Horn and Wounded Knee in the "autobiography" *Black Elk Speaks,* to Linda Hogan's dramatization of the Oklahoma oil boom in her novel *Mean Spirit,* to Simon Ortiz's exploration of the history and implications of mining in the Grants Uranium Belt in the poetry and narrative of *Fight Back: For the Sake of the People—For the Sake of the Land,* to Vine Deloria, Jr.'s challenge of the bases and tenets of Western history in essays like those from *God is Red*. Within these various literary forms, the tacks Native authors have taken also run the gamut of possibility and have included revisionist accounts, pre-emptive interpretations of contemporary historical events, "eye-for-an-eye" propagandistic distortions, attempts at completely autonomous representations, and multiple combinations of all of the above. However, the literary representations of history by Native American writers I find the most compelling and ultimately the most rewarding are those which, by their humor, work to unmask and disarm history, to expose the hidden agendas of historiography and, thereby, remove it from the grasp of the political panderers and return it to the realm of story. Among those who have approached the deadly serious business of history with trickster humor are Carter Revard, Gerald Vizenor, and Gordon Henry. Through their play and intellectual bantering they force a reconsideration of the processes and powers of historical reckoning and thus, essentially, liberate the reader from preconceived notions and incite an imaginative reevaluation of history.

Key to the ability of these writers to undertake such a liberation, is their keen awareness of the contested visions of history and their imaginative rendering of the places (both physical and intellectual) of cultural historical contact. In discussing American Literature, American Indian author and scholar Louis Owens makes an important distinction between, notions of territory (unoccupied space) and frontier (place of contact) ("Mixedblood Metaphors: Identity in Contemporary Native American Fiction"). Revard, Vizenor and Henry write works about the frontier; that is they do not proceed from the illusion of any pristine historical territory, untouched by the accounts of the opposition. Instead they draw their humor and power from an awareness of the reality of the place where the diverse accounts of history come into contact with one another. They take for granted and force recognition of the already embattled visions all readers bring to the text. Is American virgin land or widowed land? Did native peoples migrate to this continent or emerge here? Are the stories of native peoples to be classified as myth or history? Was America discovered or invaded? These authors expend little of their wit and energy to advance either of the opposing sides of these arguments; instead, they flesh out the frontier in all its immense complexity. They shift and reshift their story's perspectives, turn the tables of historical events, unmask stereotypes and racial poses, challenge the status of history's heroes and emerge somewhere in a new frontier of Indian literature, somewhere between fact and fiction, somewhere between the probable and the possible, in some border area of narrative which seems more true than previous accounts of history.

ii
"what if a much of a which of a wind"

One of the more easily analyzed moves of these writers involves perspective. By a deft twist of the popular vision of history, they submerge their readers in the "what ifs" of historical interpretation: What if the actions of history were reversed? Would this affect the moral interpretations of events? What if history's heroes were not what textbooks make them out to be? What if *white* society were envisioned as the demonic "other"? How would their actual cultural practices measure up to their professed standards of evaluation? Perhaps most fundamentally, what if things did not happen exactly as they have always been portrayed, the issues, the sides, were not as neatly drawn as they have been made out to be? And, finally, what happens to our understanding of events if we recognize the subjective quality of history?

Vizenor begins this game of reversals with the most basic assumptions about tribal origins. In the film *Harold of Orange*, when one of his characters is asked about his opinion of the Bering Strait migration theory, the character responds with his own question: "Which way?" At the confused response of his interrogator, he clarifies his question: "Which way across the Bering Strait?" The moment of humor and imbalance such a scene creates for the audience is Vizenor's wedge in, his ploy to soften their resistance to other "betrayals" of historical dogma, and a move to incite the audience's own re-reading of history.

Another of Vizenor's moves to dis-arm history reverses the perspective on the possession of remains. In a scene in *Harold of Orange*, Harold implies that the bones in a museum case may actually be, not those of an Indian, but those of a white anthropologist lost in a snow storm and later mistaken for a dead Indian. In his novel *The Heirs of Columbus*, the characters struggle for possession of the remains of both Pocahontas and Columbus. Vizenor's playful reversals in these stories challenge readers to reconsider the readily accepted treatment of the remains of "primitive" cultures as museum objects and the implied hierarchy that allows or endorses such practice. Thus Vizenor employs the Pocahontas scenes to raise issues not only about physical remains but about tribal identity as well for, as Will Roscoe notes in his review of *Heirs*, "Whoever controls the artifacts of history controls history" (11). The Pocahontas myth of American popular literature has made her into a perfect stereotype of the primitive "other," an Indian princess, emblem of the romantic past and of the primitive's adoring devotion and humble gratitude for the salvation of civilization. Vizenor moves to expose the stereotype and the motivations behind its creation and to recover the story and identity of Pocahontas, an identity and a story representative, of course, of the larger tribal culture.

Henry offers his own commentary on the museumization of culture and the appropriation of cultural identity and story in a wonderful tale of a leg which is woven throughout his novel *The Light People*.[1] Through a series of bizarre circumstances, the ceremonially dressed and amputated leg of an Anishinaabe man, Four Bears from Fineday Reservation, becomes the discovery of a young graduate student in anthropology and the pride of a metropolitan museum. Years later, when it is discovered there by Osahwa, another young man from the reservation, a legal battle for the leg ensues. In the untangling of the story of the leg, the musings of characters, and the courtroom drama, Henry tracks the passionate arguments of each side and illuminates the subtle philosophical, moral and religious implications of the actions of each of the involved parties. In a section called "Requiem for a Leg," for example, he offers this insightful lament of the museumized leg, describing it as:

> catalogued in curio stasis, as if the vanished were never meant to exist in a moment beyond the fictional situation, but were instead left to struggle with another simulated reconstruction, as invisible victims of the interpretation of artifact. (136)

In other places Henry's analysis is humorously cast as when the anthropologist of the story recounts the debate of the museum board over the significance of the leg. The various theories of the board members, those Henry later labels "Eurocentric intellectual culture-mongers and mythmakers" (179), serve to suggest the sometimes ludicrous methods of science and to raise questions about the accuracy of what is enshrined as scholarship. The odd series of interpretations they offer alternately claim the leg was "an emblem of warfare" cut off in torture and floated down the river "as a reminder to enemies"; "part of a ritual to test the manhood of warrior initiates"; "a ritual for getting rid of diseases in the community, a dream ritual in which the leg takes the diseases into the purifying waters of the river"; or part of a ritual in which "the leg is given to the rivers to insure good fishing" (173-4). Ultimately, the official museum plaque claims: "Though it is not known why the leg

---

[1] Page references given are for book manuscript and will not match forthcoming published edition.

was left like this, some scholars believe burying a leg like this in full ceremonial leg-ging was a common practice in the reservation period" (137). The predisposition of anthropology and the relegation of Indians to a romantic past are further ex-posed in Henry's story when the scholar who discovered the leg admits that "he never considered the possibility of the leg belonging to a living twentieth-century Ojibway" but had "as soon as he saw the leg" thought of "an Indian of the past" (175). Finally, the authority of the scientific community is again undermined and the scholar's motivations questioned in the story when the tribal attorney belittles the rationalizations the anthropologist offers for his actions:

> "Gee, I don't know. A leg floats to you out of nowhere, and your first thought is that no one around the village will know anything. . . I bet you saw an opportunity in the leg, a chance to capture something unique, a one of a kind find that would forever connect your name with an authentic artifact." (177)

Here and elsewhere both Henry's storyline and the rich suggestiveness of his prose compel the reader to a succession of reexaminations and reevaluations of the issues of cultural appropriation.

In this trickster vein, the work of Revard, Vizenor and Henry also derive much play from the doctrine of discovery, from the record of Columbus' declarations and the ethnocentric evaluations of native peoples in his diary, from the rhetoric of manifest destiny, and from the plethora of popular Indian stereotypes. In "Re-port to the Nation: Claiming Europe," for example, Revard turns the tables on dis-covery. From aboard a Thames excursion boat, his protagonist claims England. Stopping at gas stations throughout France to issue proclamations, he lays claim to multiple areas of that country. "Whether they understood that France now belongs to us," Revard writes, "was not clear" (167). The author thus succeeds in altering the reader's perspective of the historical rights of discovery and conquest and he incites a challenge of the validity of the European claims. In the story, he also re-calls the absurd and unfounded judgments made about Native American intelli-gence, religious practices, commerce, etc. through the equally rash evaluations made by his own protagonist (many of which echo—with a cultural twist—the de-scriptions recorded by Columbus). Revard writes, for example, that the Europeans "do not know how to use the land" and that their religious shrines "certainly have a lot of torture scenes in them, and these are the models for spiritual life they say" (169). His text also offers commentary on the many actions which result from the presumption of cultural superiority and exposes the double standard inherent in the colonial definition of civilized behavior. His "explorer," for example, reports, "It may be impossible to civilize the Europeans"; and then offers as evidence this accounting of their actions: "The Europeans kill each other pretty casually, as if by natural instinct, not caring whether they blow up women, kids or horses, and next day display the mutilated corpses on front pages or television screens" (166-67). He then proceeds to outline his own (equally violent) plan for dealing with the savage Europeans: "Possibly we could even teach the poor souls our Osage language, although if our faith and goodness can't be pounded into them we may just have to kill them all" (169), and finally predicts and justifies the outcome of the encounter: "We will , however, as the superior race, prevail in the end" (170). Thus Revard challenges one of the most basic tenets of the theory of manifest destiny—inherent moral superiority. These are but a small sampling of the passages in the satiric text which cast the discovery and its fallout in new light.

The targets of each of the authors are numerous and include general policies as well as specific military encounters and particular historic figures. But in each case, in Vizenor's satiric play in *Heirs* and *Harold of Orange*, Revard's in "Report to the Nation," and Henry's in *Light People*, their works garner their force from their reader's knowledge of historical events, documents, accounts and interpretations. By overturning the enshrined accounts of history with trickster reversals, they arouse in a reader an awareness of the way that history can and has been possessed. The intentions of the authors, however, are not to re-possess history nor to replace one historical account with another, but to incite the reader to an imaginative re-evaluation of both the accounts and the processes of history. Vizenor, for example, tells a tale in *Heirs* too fantastic to be mistaken for substitute doctrine. He claims Columbus himself descends from Mayan ancestry, claims also that "The Maya brought civilization to the savages of the Old World," and that Columbus' misdirected adventure to the Americas was a "return to his homeland" (9). He recounts the sexual union of Columbus with a tribal woman named Samana from which issues the mixedblood heirs of the novel, and generally embellishes history's staid accounts of Columbus with a wild irreverent tale of sex, gambling, intrigue over the remains of the explorer, murder and general mayhem. He caps the novel off with a new story of discovery, the discovery by the heirs of the Columbus' genetic signature of "survivance." In a final reversal, Vizenor's novel credits the explorer, whose appearance in the Americas signaled the beginning of an era of destruction of Native American cultures, with becoming the source of their survival through the healing genes of his remains. This zany trickster tale seeks to relieve the reader of the burden of historical truth. As Barbara Babcock has noted, the "excitement" of the trickster story "lies in the suggestion that any particular ordering of experience may be arbitrary and subjective" (181). Vizenor's aim is to liberate the reader from the so-called facts of history and to allow them to imagine for themselves the what-ifs of story.

iii

Righting History

But the satiric intentions and effects of Vizenor, Henry and Revard's works extend beyond the events of history to the very documents which record and fix its interpretation, and to the philosophy and politics which empower such documents. For example, the reported declarations of Christopher Columbus and his diary account are recalled to the minds of readers by Revard and Vizenor when they employ language in their fiction which simultaneously mimics and ridicules the historical documents. The account of Columbus' claiming of the West Indies reads this way:

> The Admiral called to the two captains and to the others who jumped ashore and to Rodrigo de Escobedo, secretary of the whole fleet, and to Rodrigo Sanchez of Segovia, and said that they should bear faith and witness how he before them all was taking, as in fact he took, possession of the said island for the King and Queen, their Lord and Lady, making the declarations that are required, as is set forth in the testimonies which were taken down in writing. (33)

Revard, of course, plays off this passage in "Report to the Nation." And in *Heirs*, Vizenor's recounting of the claiming of Point Assinika by the heirs of Columbus' is filled with mocking echoes:

> The Heirs of Columbus bear faith and witness that we have taken possession of this point in the name of our genes and the wild tricksters of liberties, and we made all the necessary declarations and had these testimonies recorded by a blond anthropologist. (119)

In addition to undercutting Columbus' declarations of ownership, the Vizenor passage also derides the implied authority of this and other written testimony (particularly authority claimed principally or solely on the basis of something having been recorded in writing). By specifically identifying a blond anthropologist as recorder of the testimonies, Vizenor unleashes his satiric force on two of his favorite targets—the social sciences and anthropologists. His humor works to unmask the colonialism and ethnocentric assumptions which he believes underlie the practice of Indian anthropology, particularly the practice of raising to the level of ultimate explicator recorders of culture on the single basis of their being themselves from an-"other," dominant and supposedly superior culture. Vizenor's playful challenge of such arbitrary status finds voice elsewhere in the novel when, in another deft turnabout, he essentially removes Columbus' "otherness" (and therefore, his inherent cultural status) by making Columbus himself a mixedblood and American Indian (Mayan). Of course, another of Vizenor's implied targets here is the false notion of cultural or racial purity.

Historical documents and the philosophy which empowers them also become the targets of Henry's satire in *The Light People*. A chapter entitled "The Prisoner of Haiku," through the haiku poetry of the character Elijah Cold Crow, recalls the practice in many historical documents (treaties, deeds of allotment, etc.) of representing tribal consent by an "x":

> Signatures, names, the
> undersigned, with marks and lines
> anglicized in print
>
> Clan leaders, head men
> scripted identities so
> many with an x.
>
> Andayk, Flatmouth, Sweet,
> Minogeshig, Broken Tooth,
> an x by the name. (82)
>
> Abetung he who
> inhabits his X mark
> in the presence of ——. (85)

In other haiku of Cold Crow's, Henry writes of "name energy" and identifies the "tracks of birds in dirt" as "hieroglyphs." Read together with the previous haiku, these seem to suggest the possibility of meaning in languages and signs other than those "anglicized in print" and to imply the loss or theft of "name energy" through the enforced use of English. Henry's novel contains an essay by another character, Bombarto Rose, which also analyzes—in a language imitative of the often convoluted legal documents and philosophical treatises—various implications of the representation of X: "the artificial parameters of a metaphysical residence" (89), the document as "abstract, a function of language" (90), and the collision in the document between a "static historical reference point" and an "ahistorical referent to. . .natural time" (86). Thus, through the interplay of the haiku themselves and their connections with the larger story including Rose's essay and the punishment Cold Crow suffered in boarding school for the speaking of his native language, Henry succeeds in suggesting much about the definitions of literacy and their political expediency: the dominance of the written over the oral, the privileging of English over tribal languages, and the devaluation of culture and identity which results from labels of "illiteracy."[2] The story also suggests the questionable nature of the historic documents themselves and attests to the way the historic contest has come to be at least partially symbolized in language. Henry writes of Cold Crow, for example, that something was "deeply embedded in the prisoner's history. A partial loss of language, new forms, old forms were part of his existence" (71).

For Native American authors, too, the contest has come to be symbolized in language, and has in its literary manifestation involved both old and new forms. Native peoples have recorded oral histories and created native language publications in addition to writing history and literature in English in both western and "non-standard" forms. Publications like N. Scott Momaday's *The Way to Rainy Mountain* and Leslie Silko's *Storyteller,* for example, illustrate the mixed-genre creations which refuse to honor scholarly distinctions between myth and history, history and story, autobiography and history, prose and poetry, etc. because they recognize and value the relationships among and inevitable overlapping of these categories.

The literary works of Vizenor, Revard and Henry likewise challenge in various ways the forms and methods of history, sometimes in the mock-rendering of standardized historical forms (as noted in Henry's *The Light People),* sometimes in a style deliberately anti-historical, anti-literary, or perhaps even anti-form. The work of Vizenor, for example, often replaces the honored cause and effect structure with the disarray of chance just as Henry's novel creates a cacophony of forms and a tangle of storied layers. Revard's work, too, is amass with layers and, in "Never Quite A Hollywood Star," it becomes a quagmire of shifting narrative grounds. This story, written in a metafictive mode, whips the reader back and forth between

---

[2] For a more complete discussion of the issues of literacy, please see: Kimberly M. Blaeser, "Learning 'The Languages the Presidents Speak': Images and Issues of Literacy in American Indian Literature," *World Literature Today,* Vol. 66, No. 2 (Spring 1992), 230-35.

story, reality, and the self-conscious framing of narrative. What these various re-formings of historical accounts achieve is reader awareness. Revard's meta-fictive approach, for example, succeeds in exposing the multi-directional fields of influ-ence between such factors as history, art, politics, news, life, and story. Among his subjects in "Never Quite a Hollywood Star" is Wounded Knee, the selective and slanted news coverage that surrounded the event, and how that reportage created the historical "truth" of the event:[3]

> The feature will explain that these are not real Indians. The surrounding Airborne Division soldiers, the machine guns on the APC's... their tracer bullets that come into the church at night so brilliantly shining and kill an Indian lying next to its wall, are not real either. They are, the reporter explains, a public relations exercise. ... The crows tell a different story. It is kept in a blue cage made of western skies and cannot reach *The New York Times*. Here come the press trailers and vans full of equipment pulling out of Wounded Knee. Behind them shots break out but do not exist. (220)

As another part of his move to expose the multiple range of influences on our thinking, Revard positions his fictive personae within the mind of the imaginary reader and in philosophical opposition to the reader, identifying his action as "an Indian attack." Naturally, the actual reader is then motivated to respond, most like-ly to disassociate from the thinking Revard's personae exposes as somehow faulty. Revard gives his reader a stake in the story and in history and causes the reader to discover how implicated each individual is in the telling of history. As Henry writes, "We apprehend the truth as we become part of the story" (145).

Vizenor's book *The People Named the Chippewa* (whose very title recalls the renaming of the Anishinaabeg) also has as its purpose the re-forming of history into personal story. The subtitle of the book identifies the pieces as "Narrative His-tories" which Vizenor places in opposition to linear historical accounts:

> The Anishinaabeg did not have written histories; their world views were not linear narratives that started and stopped in manifest binaries. The tribal past lived as an event in visual memories and oratorical gestures; woodland identities turned on dreams and visions. (24)

---

[3] For a similar challenge of the accuracy and methods of journalism, see Gerald Vizenor, "Sand Creek Survivors *Earthdivers: Narratives on Mixed Descent* (Minne-apolis: U of Minnesota P, 1981) 33-46. I discuss this work by Vizenor in *Gerald Vi-zenor: Writing—in the Oral Tradition* (Norman: U of Oklahoma P, forthcoming).

So in his accounts, Vizenor chooses a narrative form, he allows the historical significance of oral tradition, dreams and visions, and perhaps most significantly, he
makes a place in historical telling for imagination. E. M. Forster claimed in *Aspects
of the Novel* that "fiction is truer than history, because it goes beyond the evidence,
and each of us knows from his own experience that there is something beyond the
evidence" (63). Through the power of imagination (what Momaday called "speculation"), Vizenor attempts to "relume" the past, to bring it to life by imbuing the
evidence with suggestion, implication and possibility.[4]

"Shadows at La Pointe," as one of Vizenor's "narrative histories," displays the
multiple dimensions and multiple perspectives he strives for. In this narrative, he
clearly intends to expose the invisible seams that lie behind the apparent gloss of
history, to reveal the inevitable effects of personality on historiography and the effects of historical accounts on culture. To illustrate these interconnections, Vizenor, like Revard, employs a meta-literary technique, here a meta-historical
strategy which mimics the realistic complexity of any accurate account. He creates
a kind of house-that-jack-built effect. "Shadows at La Pointe" tells a story through
the eyes of two young mixedblood women from Madeline Island who play hooky
from school, romp in the spring weather, recall the fine stories they have heard at
the trading post, dream of their place in history, and hatch a plot to stow away on
a steamer. It at once encompasses: the events of an era, the historical story about
the events of an era, the tales that were told about the inventors who wrote the historical story of an era, the life stories of those who told the tales about those who
wrote the historical story of an era, and finally, the thoughts and dreams of those
who ultimately have their identities formed by all the previous stories. We can extend the range of the piece, the range of historical influence, yet further if, as Linda
Ainsworth suggests, the probable target audience for Vizenor's narrative histories
includes the contemporary "people named the Chippewa" whose survival Vizenor
hopes will be the next story. The survival though, Vizenor contends, depends upon
the recognition of the lie of history and the truth of imagination. For only if the
Anishinaabeg refuse to accept and be determined by the romantic linear history

---

[4] The following statement by Momaday was made as part of his contribution to a
discussion at the Library of Congress, Washington, January 1974, and published
in *Teaching Creative Writing* (Washington: Government Printing Office, 1974) 26-
64: "It is speculation which is not fact in the ordinary sense, but neither is it fiction. I believe that this speculation, which is an act of the imagination, is indis-
pensable to the writing of non-fiction prose."

which ends with the tragic death or museumization of Indian people, can they continue to imagine their place in the story of ongoing life. Therefore, the very literary style of Vizenor, Revard and Henry writes itself against the events of history and the forms of history's recounting to contest their dominance and to claim and enact liberation and healing from the past tyranny of history.

This re-forming of history into healing story is part of the repertoire and purpose of all three authors. Vizenor writes in *Heirs* about "story energy" and those "paramount healers" whose "stories and humor" become "in some way, the energy that heals" (164). Through Vizenor's new Columbus story, his other trickster tales and his narrative histories, readers in general and perhaps tribal people in particular are, like the deformed children of the *Heirs* novel, "mended in one way or another" (164). Because historical stories, imaginative stories, cultural stories work to form our identity, the disarming of history through satiric humor liberates and empowers us in the imagination of our destinies. Henry's character Rose Meskwaa talks about stereotypic images of Indian people—"the cowboy killings, the product faces"—and how "knowing the images inside can kill you and put faces on you that you can't get off" (26). But Rose used art, painting, to "turn images inside out from the mind to the hand" and, more importantly, discovered "the [new artistic] images could replay healing images inside someone" (26). Henry, Vizenor and Revard all turn old images and old forms inside out with trickster humor because they, too, know the powers of story and humor: "Humor," writes Vizenor, "has political significance" *(Heirs* 166), and "Comedy," writes Revard, "is worth more than tragedy any time where survival is at stake" ("Report" 180). So it is with survival humor that many contemporary Native Americans attempt to right history in their literary creations and "replay healing images inside" their reader's minds.

WORKS CITED

Churchill, Ward. *Fantasies of the Master Race: Literature, Cinema and the Colonization of American Indians.* Monroe, ME: Common Courage P, 1992.

Columbus, Christopher. "The Discovery of the West Indies, 12 October 1492-15 January, 1493." *The Journal of the First Voyage of Christopher Columbus* in *American Literature: A Prentice Hall Anthology, Vol. I.* Gen. Ed. Emory Elliot. Englewood Cliffs, NJ: Prentice Hall, 1991: 33-38.

Deloria, Vine, Jr. *God is Red.* New York: Dell, 1973.

———. "Forward." *New and Old Voices of Wah'kon-tah: Contemporary Native American Poetry.* Eds. Robert K. Dodge and Joseph B. McCullough. New York:

International Publishers, 1985: ix-x.

Drinnon, Richard. *Facing West: The Metaphysics of Indian-Hating and Empire-Building*. Minneapolis: U of Minnesota P, 1980.

Forster, E. M. *Aspects of the Novel*. New York: Harcourt, 1927.

Henry, Gordon. *The Light People*. Norman: U of Oklahoma P. Forthcoming.

————. "The Prisoner of Haiku." *Earth Song, Sky Spirit: Short Stories of the Contemporary Native American Experience*. Ed. Clifford Trafzer. New York: Doubleday, 1992: 63-82.

Hogan, Linda. *Mean Spirit*. New York: Atheneum, 1990.

Martin, Calvin. "An Introduction Aboard the *Fidele*." *The American Indian and the Problem of History*. Ed. Calvin Martin. New York: Oxford UP, 1987: 3-26.

Momaday, N. Scott. *The Way to Rainy Mountain*. Albuquerque: U of New Mexico P, 1969.

Neihardt, John G. *Black Elk Speaks*. Lincoln: U of Nebraska P, 1932, rpt. 1961.

Ortiz, Simon. *Fight Back: For the Sake of the People. For the Sake of the Land. INAD Journal.* (U of New Mexico.) 1.1 (1980).

Owens, Louis. "Mixedblood Metaphors: Identity in Contemporary Native American Fiction," Program for Faculty Renewal Workshop on American Indian Identity, Santa Fe, February 1993.

Revard, Carter. "Report to the Nation: Claiming Europe." *Earth Power Coming: Short Fiction in Native American Literature*. Ed. Simon Ortiz. Tsaile: Navajo Community College P, 1983: 166-81.

————. "Never Quite A Hollywood Star." *Talking Leaves: Contemporary Native American Short Stories*. Ed. Craig Lesley. New York: Dell Publishing, 1991: 217-26.

Roscoe, Will. "Columbus' Comeuppance." Rev. of *Heirs of Columbus*, by Gerald Vizenor. *San Francisco Chronicle: Review*. 4 August, 1991: 1, 11.

Silko, Leslie Marmon. *Storyteller*. New York: Seaver Books, 1981.

Slotkin, Richard. *Regeneration Through Violence: The Mythology of the American Frontier, 1600-1860*. Middletown, CT: Wesleyan UP, 1973.

Swann Brian. "Introduction: Only the Beginning." *Harper's Anthology of 20th Century Native American Poetry*. Ed. Duane Niatum. New York: Harper & Row, 1988: xiii-xxxiii.

Vizenor, Gerald. "Sand Creek Survivors." *Earthdivers: Tribal Narratives on Mixed Descent*. Minneapolis: U of Minnesota P, 1981: 33-46.

————. "Harold of Orange." Film and unpublished screenplay. Dir. Richard Weise. Minnesota Film-in-the-Cities, 1983.

————. "Shadows at Lapointe." *The People Named the Chippewa: Narrative Histories*. Minneapolis: U of Minnesota P, 1984: 37-55.

————. *The Heirs of Columbus*. Hanover, NH: Wesleyan UP, 1991.

"Temporary Visibility": Deloria on Sovereignty and AIM

Robert Allen Warrior, Stanford University

Vine Deloria, Jr. (Standing Rock Sioux) came into prominence as a writer, social critic, and political leader during the watershed events in Indian America of the 1960s and 1970s.[1] The purpose of this essay is to examine the ways in which he responded to Indian activism of the time, most specifically calls for traditionalist revival among militant nationalists connected to the American Indian Movement and other organizations.

Deloria, in his various writings and interviews from the late 1960s and early 1970s, contended that the key to an American Indian future was the return to Native ceremonies and traditions within a framework of asserting sovereignty. He was certainly not the only American Indian making such an appeal. Leaders of the American Indian Movement and others were making efforts to base their political activism in traditional culture and some of the first tradition-based substance abuse programs were under development. By now, such appeals have become commonplace.

With *God is Red* Deloria provided the first and much-needed critical reflection of questions raised by such appeals to tradition. Such revitalization, he argued, must take place in the context of a larger framework if it is not to slip into apocalyptic or dogmatic western religious assumptions. Deloria's framework had

---

[1] This essay is adapted from *Tribal Secrets; Vine Deloria, Jr., John Joseph Mathews and the Recovery of American Indian Intellectual Traditions* (forthcoming, University of Minnesota Press). I use the term "sovereignty" in a rather undefined way throughout. Central to the argument here is the contention that a definition of sovereignty should emerge from the experience of communities rather than in academic discourse.

remained consistent through a half-decade of extremely energetic American Indian activism. As American Indians and other oppressed groups were caught up in
the fervor of nationalistic and separatist politics in the early 1970s, Deloria was
asking what nationalism, self-determination, and group sovereignty could really
mean in the world of lived experience.

In many ways, the events that led to the 71-day take-over of Wounded Knee in
1973 were a fulfillment of the goals of many leaders of Deloria's generation. At the
same time these events created a set of problems that represented a realization of
the greatest fears of those leaders. When he published *Custer Died for Your Sins* in
1969, Deloria believed that "Indian people...have a chance to re-create a type of society for themselves that can defy, mystify, and educate the rest of American society" (*Custer* 268).[2] His hope, he says, was not so much to be right or wrong, but to
give a "new sense of conflict to Indian affairs" and to "bring...to the surface the
greatness that is in" American Indian people and cultures (*Custer* 268-69).

The stage was set at that point, he believed, for the emergence of just that sort
of transformation in American Indian communities. National Indian leaders had
for over a decade carefully defined an agenda that would take advantage of national
attention to minority needs without allowing themselves to be merely lumped together with other minority groups. The treaty-based nationalism of traditional
people in isolated reservation communities had begun to have an impact on young
leaders in national Indian politics. Diasporic American Indians were mobilizing to
bring issues specific to their experience onto the national scene.

Beyond the heady politics of the moment, Deloria argued, American Indians
would eventually have to capitalize on the gains made in the previous decade and
solidify the process of American Indian communities taking control of their own
destinies. The time was coming, he predicted, when the politics of confrontation
would have to end and the work of building communities would have to begin.
Even the conservative turn toward "law and order" prompted by white racist fear
of African-American militancy and moralistic fear of drugs and rock and roll were
a positive part of the American Indian struggle to Deloria, insofar as these events
were forcing Indians to withdraw into their own communities and draw on their
own cultural strength (*Custer* 267-68). Deloria was most concerned with four
parts of the puzzle that might come together to interrupt this process.

First, he was concerned that the urban-based movement would become em-

---

[2] This afterword, unfortunately, does not appear in reprint editions of the book.

broiled in reservation political battles rather than developing its own agenda, tailor-made to the needs of Natives living in diaspora. Second, he feared that dispossessed Natives would uncritically copy the tactics of Black Power. Third, he warned that media coverage of American Indian activism would turn political struggle into a circus in which activists with the most spectacular rhetoric would be the focus of attention. Finally, he worried that people in the Indian movement would lose their ability to think critically through and analyze the issues that were arising in the midst of all the political activity (*Custer* 252ff).

All of these fears were realized between 1969 and 1973. However disappointed Deloria was in the turns American Indian activism took during that time, he also realized as much as any of his writing contemporaries the critical importance of those events. First, the various sectors of the grassroots Indian movement confronted the Native establishment with the fact that their reformist tactics did not speak to large numbers of American Indian people on reservations and in urban areas. Second, the militants gravitated with ease toward traditional spiritual leaders very early on, asserting that the real power of American Indian politics would have at its center an affirmation of culture, spirituality, and tradition.

Because these militant activists were able to draw great numbers of people to their ranks, Deloria continued to support their efforts in court and in print. However valid were the charges that the militants were urban gangsters, confrontationists who refused to negotiate, and the "romantic inversion of racialism," they undeniably touched a nerve in the consciousness of American Indian people from the poorest and most alienated of backgrounds.[3]

Even as these events transpired, Deloria grappled with issues of what their actions meant for the future of American Indian sovereignty and freedom. A good example is Deloria's warning to American Indians against copying the tactics of African-American militant nationalists. This was not a matter of his thinking that African-Americans did not have a profound message to express through their cries of Black Power. Rather, he thought, that American Indians must continue the careful process of delineating their own issues from those of other groups. In doing so, he was trying to counter what he saw as the natural tendency of the dominating society and its institutions of power to see all minority problems through the lens

---

[3] Gerald Vizenor has been the most ardent writing critic of AIM. A good sample of his analysis of the movement is in *Crossbloods; Bone Courts, Bingo and other Reports*, 157-196. Vizenor's criticisms were and are shared by large numbers of people at the local level.

of African-American experience.[4]

More importantly, though, he contended that the various nationalistic groups of the late 60s had largely missed the point of what they were demanding. He sets out his criticisms of the militant power movements in several places, but most importantly in a chapter of We Talk, You Listen called "Power, Sovereignty, and Freedom." He begins the chapter by saying that the concept of power that was sweeping minority groups of the U.S. needs to be defined clearly because "where it has not been defined, activism has been substituted for power itself" (We Talk 114). "Few members of racial minority groups," he argues, "have realized that inherent in their peculiar experience on this continent is hidden the basic recognition of their power and sovereignty" (We Talk 115).

That peculiar experience, he contends, is that the U.S., through discrimination and through its historical legislation—its treaties, amendments, or statutes—recognizes the presence of discrete racial, cultural, and religious groups within its borders. The ostensible goal of that explicit acknowledgement, of course, is to somehow violate the integrity of the groups and move them into the mainstream of individual rights. Even though to Deloria this is "a quicksand of assimilationist theories which destroy the power of the group to influence it own future," acknowledgement of group status remains (We Talk 118).

American Indians, of course, have the strongest footing in this regard because of the existence of parallel institutions in American Indian communities that are federally recognized or have traditional forms of government still in place. Sovereignty, in Deloria's definition of it, requires constructive group action rather than demands for self-determination, "since power cannot be given and accepted" (We Talk 123). "The responsibility which sovereignty creates," he writes, "is oriented primarily toward the existence and continuance of the group" (We Talk 123).

The path of sovereignty, he says, is the path to freedom. That freedom, though, is not the standard, western sort of freedom which can be immediately defined and lived. Rather, the challenge is to articulate what sort of freedom as it "emerge[s] through the experience of the group to exercise the sovereignty which they recognize in themselves" (We Talk 124). Through this process-centered definition of sovereignty, Deloria is able to avoid making a declaration as to what contemporary American Indian communities are or are not. Rather, Deloria recognizes that American Indians have to go through a process of building com-

---

[4] See Deloria, Custer, 168ff. and We Talk, You Listen; New Tribes, New Turf, 86ff.

munity and that that process would define the future.

What Deloria articulates, then, is a position that does not simply posit the essential superiority of American Indian traditions over other ways of life and cultures. His argument for American Indian traditions being the best way of living comes from the presence of those traditions in this particular place for such a long period of time and because of the actual practices derived from them. At the same time, he points to many other groups in the U.S.—the Nation of Islam, the Amish, the Acadians of Louisiana—that have managed to create and sustain a sovereign identity (*We Talk* 129,133).

In doing so, Deloria is pointedly humanistic in asserting that we must evaluate our situation based on what humans have created and how they have created it. He also advocates a position that is not merely a call for the U.S. to break down into tribes closed off from the rest of the world. Rather, he recognizes that the withdrawal of a group to draw on its own resources does not cut it off from the fact that other groups influence its future. And, he argues that humans of different cultures need to have the positive experiences of culture affirmation while at the same time they need to confront a set of challenges for which no culture has all answers. Evaluating various perspectives requires speaking of the actual practices and processes involved.

The necessity of discussing sovereignty in terms of actual practices, according to Deloria, comes from confronting a system that abstracts principles in order to impose its will on others. "Can we," he asks, "continue to struggle for justice on an atomistic premise that society is merely a conglomerate of individuals who fall under the same laws?" (*We Talk* 106). His answer, of course, is no. At the same time, though, groups do little by demanding that the dominating society change. Instead, Deloria advocates building communities and social structures through which those communities exercise political, economic, and spiritual power along with responsibility.

Yielding to the temptation to lash out at the oppressor, according to Deloria, is to be avoided not for humanistic reasons or to avoid the backlash that such actions always produces. Rather, such actions keep the various groups from exercising the power that they already possess. This power, Deloria argues, is not only the positive material of their cultural and political lives that they have been able to maintain over years of oppression, but also in the "persecution of a group because it is a group" (*We Talk* 117).

In coming together to demand self-determination and sovereignty, he argues, groups were undertaking the first steps toward finding an alterative to the false consciousness and praxis of individualism in the U.S. What was lacking in these demands, however, was a realization that the dominating society had already acknowledged the existence of the group, even if in doing so it violated its own mythologies of the primacy of individual rights and property ownership.

What Deloria had to contend with as he criticized the power movements was that the extreme, nationalist message of militant activists was able to awaken within American Indians the kind of consciousness through which large numbers of people rise up to take their destinies into their own hands. In the afterword to *Custer* he had said that he "wants to search out the sheep missing from our national Indian fold." His goal in doing so, he continues, would be to "help them get moving with the rest of the tribes" (*We Talk* 278). As the actions of the 1970s unfolded, those lost sheep multiplied into the myriad Indian voices, some in the fold, many outside of it, that remain to this day.

The combination of diasporic anger and reservation-based traditional people created tremendous energy that the leaders from the National Congress of American Indians and even the National Indian Youth Council had never been able to tap into. Further, they provided an alternative for the poorest and least visible American Indians. As the presence of these new voices and experiences grew in number, strength, and vocality, Deloria concomitantly contended that the framework of sovereignty that he had argued for in 1969 was still basically sound. Without this framework, he feared, tradition-based revitalization would not be able to respond adequately to the political, economic, and social necessities of American Indian communities.

The return to tradition cannot in Deloria's analysis be an unchanging and unchangeable set of activities, but must be part of the life of a community as it struggles to exercise sovereignty. While dressing up in beads and feathers provided a successful means of gaining media attention and funding from progressives and churches, it did not get at the deeper issues of how viable, responsible communities could emerge in Indian country.

Tradition is limited in this way, he argued, because it was not originally developed to confront the particular challenges of contemporary American Indian communities and politics. A contemporary American Indian politics would have to grapple, he argued, with a situation that made demands that required the creation of new categories of existence and experience. He sums this up in an interview when he says,

Everyone doesn't have to do everything that the old Indians did in order to have a modern Indian identity. We don't have to have every male in the tribe do the Sun Dance. We need a larger variety of cultural expression today. I don't see why Indians can't be poets, engineers, songwriters or whatever. I don't see why we can't depart from traditional art forms and do new things. Yet both Indians and whites are horrified when they learn than an Indian is not following the rigid forms and styles of the old days. That is nonsense to me but it has great meaning to a lot of people who have never considered the real meaning of cultural change and national development. (McKale 50)

To understand what the "real meaning" of traditional revitalization is, then, American Indians must realize that the power of those traditions is not in their formal superiority, but in their adaptability to new challenges.

After Wounded Knee, Deloria's criticisms of the militant movement were very pointed even though he supported the action in court and in print. By then, he felt, the Indian movement had lost any sense of pragmatism and had replaced their own place-centered traditions with an "eschatological vision" similar to that of the Ghost Dancers 83 years earlier. "The movement of today," he says in comparing the Wounded Knee takeover to the Ghost Dance, "asserts the cultural superiority of Indian traditions over those of Anglo-Saxon peoples. The inherent superiority will, it is alleged, become historically manifest" ("Religion" 14). In arguing thus, he continues his warning against falling into the trap of an idealism that loses its sense of pragmatism.

What the traditionalist-urban militant movement had not yet decided, according to Deloria, was how they would deal with the new, offensive situation in a way constant with Indian traditions. Because they had practiced sovereignty through traditional ceremonies and social relationships, the traditionals were in a much better position to confront the needs of communities than were the tribal councils whose primary interests were economic (Deloria, "Religion" 15). In other words, the traditionalists represented the emergence of a neglected perspective that held much promise, but was not the answer in and of itself.

The struggle for freedom, then, could not be a matter simply of dressing up in the trappings of the past and making demands. Deloria pointed out that those who turn tradition into idols fail to understand the real power of those traditions. "Truth," as previously quoted, "is in the ever changing experiences of the community. For the traditional Indian to fail to appreciate this aspect of his own heritage is the saddest of heresies. It means that the Indian has unwittingly fallen into the trap of western religion" ("Religion" 15).

To summarize, Deloria's experience of being the most prolific commentator on American Indian activism in the early 1970s produced his particular views on the role tradition can and should play in the development of an American Indian future. First, he contended, the affirmation of tradition provides the necessary raising of consciousness among those who have been taught that the ways of their ancestors were barbaric, pagan, and uncivilized. Second, tradition provides the critical constructive material upon which a community rebuilds itself.

Within this process, though, Deloria points out that tradition cannot be placed upon an idolatrous pedestal. Further, the changes that centuries of oppression have wrought upon those traditions must be taken into consideration in finding the wisest path toward a sovereign future. His comments during this time predicted the best of what has happened in the time since Wounded Knee in many reservation communities. Though the antagonisms among different groups remain, community-based activists and leaders have made movement toward bringing together tradition and pragmatic politics in such areas as substance abuse, tribal government, and education.

After Wounded Knee, the leaders of AIM spent most of their time in court or hiding as fugitives. They, in Deloria's words, "understand the gut issues that people of reservation communities and in the cities really care about.... They can rally a high percentage of people in any Indian community because they are really at the same place mentally and emotionally as those people are"[5] (McKale 52).

At one level, then, Deloria understood that AIM and other aggressive, militant groups had achieved mass support greater than earlier national Indian organizations had. At another level, though, he was concerned that the heat of the moment had guided Native activism into losing its sense of historical perspective and becoming a victim of its own success. With the movement "stalled in its own rhetoric" and no longer able to capture national attention, the conservatives and moderates on the national Indian scene found themselves reaping the greatest benefits of the often-courageous actions of AIM and the traditionals (Deloria, "Religion" 30; Forbes 124).

What the various movements were not overcoming, however, was the critical problem of how much of what they did played into the expectations of the dominating society. As Deloria writes of the increased attention he and other authors were receiving, "every book on modern Indian life [has been] promptly buried by

---

[5] McKale, Interview, 52.

a book on the 'real' Indians of yesteryear" (*God* 44). He goes on to analogize as to what would have happened if African-Americans received this same sort of debilitating exclusive fascination from non-Indians during their freedom struggle in the Civil Rights and Black Power movements (*God* 46-49). He has reporters asking Martin Luther King, Jr. "about the days on the old plantation," deciding that he is a "troublemaker," and concluding "that everything will be all right if the blacks would simply continue to compose spirituals" (*God* 46). He goes on to imagine the March on Washington being eclipsed by a new best-selling book, "*Bury My Heart at Jamestown*," that convinces white readers "to vow never again to buy and sell slaves" (*God* 47).

He goes on to comment on the increasing popularity of Native American imagery in the environmental movement and in popular culture and the growing number of books featuring words of wisdom from 19th century Indians and sepia-toned photographs. As he says, "Anthologies of spirituals become very popular, ... sternly inform[ing] us we must come to understand the great contributions made by slaves to our contemporary culture. 'More than ever,' one commentary reads, 'the modern world needs the soothing strain of "Sweet Chariot" to assure us that all is well'" (*God* 48). These cultural dynamics that seem ridiculous in the African-American situation not only dominated the Native activist movement, Deloria asserts, but, "a substantial portion of the public yearned for it to happen" (*God* 49).

Playing into these dynamics, according to Deloria, obscured deeper questions that the earlier generation had attempted to confront. These more cynical, harsh criticisms come, for the most part, in less public, non-Native audience forums. "The deeper question," Deloria argues, "is really about how one becomes or remains an Indian in the 20th century. A lot of the action is to return only to the external, show-business image of Indians, to wear feathers, long hair, dance and sing, and act mean all the time" (McKale 50). Thus, the pride and consciousness engendered by the militant actions was bought at a price. Calling Wounded Knee a "sorry melodrama" that was problematic because "it is clothed in the symbols of yesteryear," Deloria says,

> The widespread Indian failure to comprehend the experiences of the immediate past is matched by the inability of whites to relate to the modern Indian.... Whites look at the most profound and sacrificial efforts of contemporary Indians and find them wanting because they, the whites, can only relate to the Indians of the past they come to know through movies and television. Confrontation on the level of ideas becomes impossible, and misunderstanding abounds. Indians have won a temporary visibility with the media recognition of their problems. The

price of that victory for all of us was the missed opportunity to understand the nature of the deep gulf separating Indian and non-Indian. ("Religion" 13-14)

Importantly, Deloria's criticism here and in other places is not that direct action or even violence are intrinsically wrong, but that any political activism must bring with it critical reflection and constructive strategy.

He echoes this sentiment in another evaluation of the Native and other activism of the time that had "forever altered our lives" by saying, "The bitterness of reflection these days dwells not on what was accomplished but on what could have been accomplished had [people] been reasonable, just, or even consistent with themselves" ("Non-Violence" 4). In perhaps his most cynical comment of the time, he says, "the most profound message we can manage is that history teaches nothing and [humans] learn little from generation to generation.... It would seem that Indians and whites were somehow destined to be each others' victims...and perhaps that is what we must ultimately live with" ("Indian" 112).

Deloria's consistent discussion of sovereignty as an open-ended process has not been often paralleled among contemporary American Indian intellectuals. And his straightforward warning against making the rhetoric of sovereignty and tradition a final step rather than a beginning one remains an important reminder to those who engage in community, federal, and other American Indian work.

WORKS CITED

Deloria, Vine Jr. *Behind the Trail of Broken Treaties; An Indian Declaration of Independence.* New York: Delacorte P, 1974.

____. "Civilization and Isolation." *North American Review* 263 (2 Summer 1978): 11-4.

____. "Completing the Theological Circle: Civil Religion in America." *Religious Education* 71 (3 1976): 278-87.

____. *Custer Died for Your Sins; An American Indian Manifesto.* New York: Macmillan, 1969.

____. *God is Red.* New York: Grosset and Dunlap, 1973.

____. *God is Red; A Native View of Religion,* 2nd ed. Golden, Co.: North American P, 1992.

____. "Indian Affairs 1973: Hebrews 13:8." *North American Review* (Winter 1973): 108-112.

____. "The Indian Movement: Out of a Wounded Past." *Ramparts* 13 (March 1975): 28-32.

____. "Non-Violence in American Society." *Katallagete* 5 (2 Winter 1974): 4-7.

____. "Out of Chaos." *Parabola* 10 (2 May 1985): 14-22.

___. "Religion and Revolution among American Indians," *Worldview* 17 (1 January 1974): 12-15.

___. "The Theological Dimension of the Indian Protest Movement." *Christian Century* 90 (19 September 1973): 912-14.

___. *We Talk, You Listen; New Tribes, New Turf.* New York: Macmillan, 1971.

Forbes, Jack. *Native Americans and Nixon: Presidential Politics and Minority Self-Determination, 1969-1972.* Los Angeles: U of California-American Indian Studies Center, 1981.

McKale, Michael. "From Reservation to Global Society: American Culture, Liberation and the Native American: An Interview with Vine Deloria, Jr." *Radical Religion* 2 (4 1976): 49-58.

Vizenor, Gerald. *Crossbloods; Bone Courts, Bingo, and Other Reports.* Minneapolis: University of Minnesota P, 1990.

AMERICAN MYTH: OLD, NEW, YET UNTOLD

ROBERT BERNER

Myth holds a people together and gives them purpose and direction. We may say, therefore, that to the extent that America is socially and culturally fragmented we may be a people without a myth. But the truth is that we always have had a myth—that associated with the ideals of democracy, freedom, and in particular freedom of economic enterprise— and it informs, and is informed by, what Robert Bellah has called America's civil religion. Intellectuals may think there is no such myth, social critics may say that we have not lived up to it, but they must explain why our popular culture constantly refers to "the American dream" and why it has been possible for civil rights to be enhanced in the second half of this century. Surely a minority could not have achieved school desegregation and equality at the polls without reminding the majority of its mythic beliefs.

But if that is the American myth, then somewhere between that myth and the American historical record lies legend, which resembles the record in its cast of characters but also resembles the myth in originating in the aspirations rather than in the intellectual courage of the public. That cast of characters includes names both famous and less known, but it also includes figures who are only symbolic, most if not all of them cardboard cut-outs erected only to be knocked down. The American Indian, for example, has been seen both as the "red devil" who interfered savagely with the progress of the pioneers and as the "blood brother" who preferred peace to war and by implication assisted in the military defeat of his own people. Both of them informed Cooper's fictional division of an entire race into "good" and "bad" Indians. Later in the nineteenth century when the Indian was defeated and the American public could pause to consider, the assumption that the Indian was "the vanishing American" was morally convenient while lending support to the racist assumptions that had fueled the military campaign in the first place.

The Indian component in American legend has always required many euphemistic dodges. One-sided skirmishes have been called massacres when the Indians won and battles when they lost. The basic elements of the defeat of Custer's command, for example, have always been known: what happened in 1876 was not a massacre but, considering Custer's conduct on the Washita in 1868, the prevention of a massacre by Indians who out-fought or at least outnumbered Custer's force. It is thus remarkable that it has taken so long for his foolish end to be called the Battle of Little Big Horn rather than "the Custer massacre."

Clearly language is corrupted by the propagation of legends which do not jibe with the facts of history, and a corrupt terminology continues the further debasement of historical understanding—in rather the same way that political language, as George Orwell described it in a famous essay, corrupts politics and is corrupted by it. But the fashionable nonsense which presently permeates so much discussion of texts in our universities hardly can be said to improve on this process. Of course it is true that readers of historical texts too often believe only what they want to believe. But this sorry situation hardly justifies the assumption that a historical text, like any other, is a subject only for its "deconstruction," substituting for the word-created subjectivity of the writer the word-created subjectivity of the reader. The result of such an enterprise can only be the denial that there is such a thing as a historical fact outside the text upon which anything in the text depends. Or, to put it another way, if this denial is permitted, Orwell's horrible future has arrived and history is what an academic "Big Brother" says it is.

But we cannot remake the past without corrupting language, and we should remember that Orwell's imagined totalitarian state's requirement of "Newspeak" required at the same time the absolute destruction of the traditional and common-sense assumption that historical truth is possible.

A convenient starting point for investigating the way American Indians have understood the American past is the report prepared in 1970 by Rupert Costo and Jeannette Henry on their examination of three hundred American history textbooks to determine how well, according to their criteria, the full complexity of American Indian history and culture was presented. Though none of these books met their standards, no one can quarrel with their criteria, which can be understood as addressing three basic requirements: factual accuracy, recognition of the cultural significance of American Indian peoples, and a fair description of the reality of present-day Indian life. Is the history of the American Indian understood as part of American history as a whole? Is American Indian culture seen as a still organic process? Are American Indian contributions to the world and the condition of the present-day Indian taken into account? And so on.

Obviously Costo and Henry's questions point in the right direction. But in the more than two decades since they asked them we have seen the appearance of new legends which have corrupted efforts to reach an understanding of what really happened in the European conquest of America. Scholarly interest in the Indian has provided many writers, Indian and non-Indian, with the opportunity to ratify their own political and cultural assumptions. Our new "ethnohistorians," for example, have argued that colonial observers only noted those aspects of Indian life that confirmed their own presuppositions, and yet ethnohistorical conclusions often seem to suggest that they also can see only the Indian they want to see. Kirkpatrick Sale's account of the Columbian encounter, *The Conquest of Paradise,* may or not provide a useful corrective in belittling everything European, but it seems to be inspired by a strident environmentalism in the name of an Indian ideal of living with the land which, given the last five centuries, cannot be realized. And as John Daniels has pointed out, the remarkable increase in estimates of the pre-Columbian population of the Americas—and thus of the extent of the slaughter of most of it even before permanent settlements had been achieved in what is now the United States—accompanied the rise in the Vietnam "body count": "we" were slaughtering non-white people in Vietnam just as "we" slaughtered them in the sixteenth century.

The use of *genocide* as a label for the destruction of much of the pre-Columbian population is an example of the way the corruption of language and the manipulation or even invention of historical fact go hand in hand. Consider, for example, *The Missions of California: A Legacy of Genocide,* another book edited by Costo and Henry, which appeared in the context of the Vatican's consideration of Father Juniperro Serra for sainthood. The editors and their writers argue that Serra should not be canonized because his disruption of Indian culture and society in the creation of the California missions was genocidal. They actually compare the mission system with Nazi Germany and the culpability of Serra with that of the Nazi defendants in the Nuremberg trials. But *genocide,* coined in 1944 to describe the Nazi attempt to exterminate the Jews, refers specifically to the mass killing of the people of a group by a perpetrator who *intends* to destroy the group, and as James Axtell has pointed out, it does not cover those killed in a two-sided war, even if the sides are unequal, or a natural or unintended disaster such as an epidemic of disease or by individuals acting *outside* the orders of any political authority or state

(Beyond 1492, 261). When we hear the Spanish regime in the West Indies condemned for enslaving Indians while waging genocide on them by means of disease, we ought to remember that it was obviously in the slave-master's interest to keep his slaves alive if he could, that that interest eliminates any *deliberate* intention to wipe them out, that a true genocidal campaign must be *planned,* and that in any case smallpox and other diseases were as great a mystery and almost as great a problem for the Spanish as they were for the Indians. Axtell makes the point that except for a few episodes—the campaign against the Pequods in 1637, that of the French against the Foxes in the 1730's, or for that matter that of the Iroquois against the Hurons in 1649—there are few examples of true genocide in the history of the conquest of North America *(Beyond 1492,* 261). When we muddle the terminology, therefore, we trivialize the Jewish Holocaust and very likely cause many readers who might otherwise be outraged over the plight of the Mission Indians to drop the subject.

If the Costo-Henry volume were an isolated phenomenon we could ignore it. But rhetorical use of *genocide* and *holocaust* was pervasive in the context of preparations for recognizing the five hundredth anniversary of the first Columbus voyage. Paula Gunn Allen, for example, in her introduction to an anthology of short stories by American Indian women, selected and sometimes bent to meet her own feminist requirements, speaks of "a brutal holocaust that seeks to wipe us out," claims that in twenty-five years in the nineteenth century "millions" of Indians were slaughtered in the American West, and frequently doesn't even get the names right (2, 12). Such loose talk inevitably trivializes not only the murder of six million Jews but also the fate of real victims who died at places like Sand Creek and Wounded Knee.

But it is not likely that anything can be done to save these terms from those who use them to describe anything they dislike in the way their group is being treated. The problem remains with the substitution of legend for history, and the Spanish "black legend" is evolving into a larger European (and white American) black legend.

The tendency toward the creation of new legends in our revisionist era not only produces claims for European and white American villainy. Anyone who thinks that every evil done in the last five centuries must be European and white will also find it easy to assume that anything of value that has been accomplished must be less European and white than conventional history has suggested. An example is the frequently repeated claim, considered proven by most Indians, that the United States Constitution was directly influenced by the structure of the Iroquois League. Molly Brant, in Maurice Kenny's poetic reconstruction of her life, addresses the Founding Fathers:

> If I could scratch figures
> I would show you the fathers of Thirteen Fires ...
> how you took up the wisdom
> of our great and wise Peacemaker.....
> If you would listen ...
> you would remember always
> where your freedoms and liberties
> first captured your attention. (130)

We must not quarrel too much with this; it is after all the speech of a character in a poem, not the thought of the historical Molly Brant but of the Molly Brant of Kenny's imagination and thus not subject to the rules of historical evidence. Still the historical inaccuracy which prompts it must be noted.

The assumption that our freedoms—meaning, I take it, those guaranteed by the Bill of Rights—originated in the Iroquois system of government must be based on the assumption that the League structure inspired the federal system defined in the Constitution and thus made the Bill of Rights possible. In fact the structure of matriarchal clans and League council and that council's parliamentary procedures bear no resemblance whatever to the structure of the Constitution. In a diatribe against the United States government the Mohawk poet Peter Blue Cloud admitted this at the same time that he made the conventional claim:

> Talk about ... this so-called United States government. A lot of it is based on the Six Nations, but they left out all the important parts like the Clan Mothers, like the Council of Elders, like the Chiefs ....If they'd really chosen wise men to run the country and women to be behind them like the Clan Mothers, ... maybe it would have worked. (Bruchac 37)

The truth, of course, is that if all that is left out, there *is* no "lot of it" in the United States Constitution that was "based on the Six Nations."

Scholars who have argued for an Iroquois influence on the Founding Fathers have cited a variety of eighteenth-century American political thinkers whose references to Indian government often seem more rhetorical than substantive, and they place considerable weight upon coincidence. Donald Grinde, in a recent summary of the arguments, cites a statement by John Adams to the effect that "Every nation in North America has a king, a senate, and a people" (a dubious claim in itself) to justify his own assertion that the structure of "king," sachems, and council is evidence of an Indian "wisdom of balance and separation of powers in American Indian governments." For Grinde, the Constitution derives from "American Indian notions of confederation, federalism, separation of powers, and the unification of vast geographic expanses under a noncolonial government ..." (164, 166). But one Indian scholar who apparently believes the Iroquois legend, Vine Deloria, Jr., commenting upon Elisabeth Tooker's arguments against Iroquois influence, denounced her scholarship because, he said, she knew so little about eighteenth-century political philosophy that she thought that Locke, rather than Montesquieu, was the greater influence on the Founding Fathers. Of course, he is right about Montesquieu, and Grinde's "American Indian notions" are actually those addressed in those writings of Montesquieu which most influenced the Constitutional convention. In other words, Deloria has missed the crucial point: if Montesquieu, not Locke, was the primary influence on the Constitution, then the Iroquois were not.

On the other hand, though Bruce Johansen's argument that the relation of the "younger" Iroquois nations (Cayuga, Oneida) to the "older" (Mohawk, Seneca) "somewhat resembled that of a two-house congress in one body ..." (25) seems rather limp, his claims for generally Indian influences on the development of American notions of political freedom proceed from a premise which is worth considering. It is that the creation of the colonial society out of which the United States emerged was from the beginning the result of the inter-penetration of European and Indian elements and that this process continued as Indian and white American (and he might have added African American) elements merged to produce the larger American culture which we know.

One aspect of this process of inter-penetration is to be seen not only in the fact that an Indian element has been pervasive in our literature from the beginning but that Indian writers, at least in part, inevitably depend for their understanding of the Indian role in American history on the work of non-Indian scholars. For this reason it is rather dismaying to read Peter Blue Cloud's contemptuous dismissal of the pioneering work of Lewis Henry Morgan. In an interview he dismissed Morgan's *League of the Iroquois* as worthless, particularly when compared to Edmund Wilson's journalistic *Apologies to the Iroquois,* which, he said, was superior because it was based on interviews with living Iroquois (Bruchac 36). Actually Blue Cloud seems not to have read either book because he did not seem to realize that Morgan inevitably based his description of the League on interviews with Iroquois and that

Wilson's book was a product not only of his investigation of modern Iroquois circumstances but of his reading of many books, including Morgan's.

We ought never to forget that historical sources are employed most legitimately—by Indian writers or any other—for artistic rather than for political or moralistic purposes. N. Scott Momaday's use, in writing *The Way to Rainy Mountain,* of Kiowa traditions as he found them in one of his sources, James Mooney's *Calendar History of the Kiowa,* and the scholarship which gives James Welch's *Fools Crow* its historical authenticity are examples. But if we cannot quarrel with Maurice Kenny's fictitious Molly Brant repeating the Iroquois legend about the Constitution, his "Glossary," presumably included in his book to provide accurate revisions of conventional history, must be judged according to historical evidence. It includes, for example, a harsh view of George Washington, who, he says, "took particular pleasure in burning Indian villages and storehouses during the American Revolution" (203). This off-hand remark hardly does justice to the complexity of the case and ignores the facts: no Indian village was burned during the Revolution by any force directly commanded by Washington; those Iroquois whose war-making power he sent Sullivan to destroy were, after all, allied to the enemies of his cause. Moreover, no record exists to indicate that he took any pleasure from Sullivan's success that was not merely political and strategic.

When we study the early history of Europe's encounter with America, we would do well to understand what really happened in the beginning. Small groups of Europeans landed on American shores and encountered small or sometimes rather large groups of Indians. The peacefulness of these first encounters were, in fact, as often as not due to the fact that these first settlers were vastly out-numbered by those they encountered. But subsequent increases in the population of the invaders made war inevitable. And the wars were not always one-sided. That fought by the Virginians against the Powhatan Confederacy was, if anything, one-sided in the other direction, and in 1622 the Indians very nearly wiped out the colony. The Europeans in any case understood what they were doing in the light of their recent experience at home—the centuries-long Spanish *reconquista* of Moorish territory, the English wars against the wild Scots and Irish and their colonization of the conquered territories. As the continent was subdued, economic realities affected the way Indian tribes formed alliances with each other or with the invaders. When, for example, the Iroquois found that they had become dependent on European trade goods (particularly guns, powder, and shot) and that they had trapped out their own territory, they inevitably became an imperialist power, pursuing bloody wars with the Hurons, the Eries, the Illinois, and other tribes. The English and the French were for a hundred years at war with a number of small powers in North America, allied with others, and at war with each other for the reason that "civilized" nations usually go to war—for profound geopolitical interests, or, to put it simply, for loot and conquest.

The truth is that the records of all nations reveal similar responses to historical circumstances. What the Iroquois did to their neighbors, what the English and French did to theirs and to each other in North America, and what Americans did in the West in the nineteenth century is what the Anglo-Saxons did to the Britons in the latter half of the fifth century and what the Normans did to the Anglo-Saxons in 1066.

What is required, in other words, is mutual understanding and a recognition of a common humanity in the records of nations which reveal origins and developments which are more alike than we may wish to believe. The assumption that Indians did not know how to scalp their enemies until Europeans taught them how to do it, for example, implies that Indians were noble savages too innocent to have figured out anything like scalping without being led astray by evil Europeans. But we ought to remember that the idea that civilization corrupts and that savagery is too innocent a state to be really savage is much older than Rousseau. In another version it informs the description of the ancient Germans in the writings of Tacitus. Those Germans were hardly more advanced socially, culturally, and politically than most Indian tribes in 1492 (and were less advanced than some), and we will come nearer to the truth if we remember that the origins of *all* nations are in "savagery." Were the Germans of Tacitus too "noble" to scalp? If so, when did their descendants take up scalping so that it could be passed on to Indians later? And who taught those descendants? And in any case why did Indians take to it so easily?

Or consider the question of Iroquois torture of prisoners. Costo and Henry more or less imply that it may never have occurred: "Examining the original sources, we find ... that they are usually dependent on the Jesuit relations" (*Textbooks* 169). And in another context they say that the Jesuit reports were "phonied up for adaptation to the original Catholic concept of the Indian as a subhuman being ..." (*Textbooks* 154). But this hardly reflects Jesuit assumptions, and certainly the Roman Catholic church settled the question in favor of Indian humanity relatively early in the Spanish experience in the West Indies, long before French Jesuits first visited the Iroquois. If we want a true account of this phenomenon, we ought not to waste time impugning Jesuit motives. Those Jesuits who witnessed burnings at the stake were appalled less by the horror of it—their doctrine, after all, had prepared them to confront human depravity—than by what they considered the trivial (that is, political, military, or merely social, rather than religious) motives of the executioners. After all, if the Iroquois burned prisoners at the stake they were only doing what was being done at the same time to religious heretics and witches in many parts of Europe. The fact is that the past of no nation will bear much examination by those who are looking for saints among their ancestors.

In this muddle of incomplete myth and false legend—to say nothing of incredible public ignorance of history—what is needed is a great exercise in syncretism if not by our people, then at least by our intellectuals, who allegedly are smarter, if not wiser, than the public at large. What is obviously wrong with the American democratic myth is that it is too EuroAmerican, which is to say that it is narrowly progressive, it is oriented only toward the future, it ignores the claims of the past and thus denies tragedy, and it reveals no interest whatever in the fate of those who were defeated to make possible what believers in the myth consider progress. We would do well to remember Walt Whitman's willingness—in "Song of Myself"—to chant a song not only for the victors but for the vanquished. We have been able to make a place in our pantheon of heroes for Robert E. Lee because we have recognized his nobility in defeat. We must do the same for our Indian heroes. As Alexander Adams says in his biography of Geronimo, the spirit of the Apaches "lives wherever men and women are struggling against overwhelming odds for freedom and justice. We, as Americans, should be proud that the Apaches' story is part of our country's heritage" (23).

The current definition of "multi-ethnicity" seems to be modelled on broadcasters' "equal time" rules. If an American literature survey course is not to be damned as "Eurocentric" it must include components for each of several racial minorities. Obviously we ought to embrace any effort to recognize contributions of individual Indians and African Americans to our history and culture. But the fragmentation of the canon of American literature gives too often a sense that there *is* no American literature, that what instead must be studied are several mutually exclusive literatures, and that the American past is not a history of a people but of several peoples in confrontations that have not been and cannot be resolved. Obviously we need to admit that the American democratic myth is narrowly Euro-American, but such an admission is without value if it does not lead to a greater wisdom in discovering the complex interrelationship of European, Indian (and African) America. From the beginning the European's consciousness was affected by the Indian as much as the Indian's was affected by the European. And though some tribes have maintained much of their traditional culture, no tribal culture is what it was in 1492 or even a hundred years ago. First Europe and then European America have happened to Indian America for five hundred years because Europe and Indian America (and African America) have happened to all of us.

To attempt to understand this process we might consider one symbolic figure, one model for the way Indians adapted to the circumstances of the European invasion, and one example of the pitfalls that await the scholar who seeks to understand the Americanization of America.

Squanto, who encountered the Pilgrims at Plymouth in 1620, had been carried to Spain as a slave by a passing English ship six years before. But he was freed through the good offices of Spanish friars, reached England, where he was employed by a London merchant, and eventually managed to return home, where he found that European disease had killed off his tribe. Bradford tells us that the Pilgrims were confounded by the appearance first of Samoset, who had acquired broken English from fishermen in "the eastern parts" (Maine), and then of Squanto, who served as their interpreter and taught them to use fish as fertilizer in their fields of maize (110-112, 115-116). He may well have learned this trick in Europe. Here we have a figure of great symbolic significance: an English-speaking, well-travelled Indian who taught Europeans how to raise an Indian grain by what may have been European methods. Our difficulty in separating Indian and European elements in our history is present from the beginning.

A model of the Indian's adaptation to the new circumstances created by the European invasion is seen in James Axtell's explanation of why early English and, in particular, French missionaries had such success in persuading Indians to convert to Christianity. Beyond the practical considerations—political or military alliances, economic aid, trade advantages—the individual Indian, Axtell says, was able simply to add Christian elements to his traditional religious notions by a syncretic process which insured that the latter could survive by taking on the protective coloration of the religion of the invader (*After Columbus* 54, 117-118). Such a strategy ought to be remembered when we attempt to discover the truth about Black Elk's conversion to Roman Catholicism almost half a century before his death and his life-time allegiance to the terms of the great vision which he experienced at the age of nine—as well as the use of that vision by John G. Neihardt in *Black Elk Speaks*. Was his conversion and his Christian practice thereafter an act of social deception? Or did he resurrect an old Lakota faith for Neihardt's benefit? Or, what is more likely, was he able to embrace Christianity because he saw in it essential similarities to Lakota religion and to his own great personal vision? Did he, in other words, maintain his traditional faith by embracing a new one? However we answer these questions, they make clear the great complexity in the question of European and American Indian cultural relations.

The traps which await anyone who seeks to understand the interpenetration of European and Indian elements in America are many. Their kind can be exemplified in the comparison which the Italian scholar Elemire Zolla makes between accounts of the Plains Indian sun dance in books by Chief Buffalo Child Long Lance and Luther Standing Bear. Zolla finds no "touch of supernatural life" in Standing Bear and condemns him for "demean(ing) himself as a white man might," whereas he believes that Long Lance's account, though it is second hand, "gives an impression of truthfulness ..." (246). But Zolla could not know Donald B. Smith's biography of Sylvester Clark Long, who called himself Long Lance and did have some Indian ancestors but certainly was not the Blackfoot he claimed to be. And if Standing Bear is not adequately "supernatural" to satisfy Zolla, he was certainly a full-blood Sioux. If Zolla is right about the authenticity of the Indian supernaturalism of Long Lance, who was hardly an Indian at all, and the lack of it in Standing Bear, who certainly was, then clearly the question of how Indian and non-Indian elements in American culture interrelate is complex.

The definition of the syncretic process of American cultural history remains the greatest challenge to modern American scholarship. Such a history might well partake of the quality of what Northrop Frye, though he did not coin the term, has called "metahistory." Most historians assume that poetry and history are two different things: they employ the distinction made by Aristotle to the effect that history is limited to what actually happened, while poetry tells us what, given the premises of the work, *ought* to happen; and they assume that whatever is "poetic" in a work of history destroys its value as history. But the writer of "metahistory" finds the poetry in history, and in this respect "metahistory" takes on some of the quality of myth: " ... when a historian's scheme gets to a certain point of comprehensiveness it becomes mythical in shape" (53).

Frye cites Gibbon, Spengler, and Toynbee as writers of comprehensive, "metahistorical" history and defines its four modes as romantic (the quest for the perfection of a classless society or the city of God), comic (progress through an evolutionary process), tragic (the decline and fall of nations), or ironic (recurrence and casual catastrophe). Gibbon and Spengler are clear examples of the tragic mode (54). Toynbee, though Frye does not say so, wrote ironic "metahistory," and Marx, to the extent that he *was* a historian, wrote in the romantic mode. The comic mode is particularly significant in American historiography because of the example of George Bancroft. Deriving his moral ardor from his Puritan traditions and his political ideals from Jacksonian democracy, Bancroft narrated the development of ideals of American liberty from the original settling of America to the writing of the Constitution in the light of assumptions about a divine plan. Providence in his view assured appropriate conditions for the planting of free institutions in America and the achievement of democracy's "city upon a hill." Certainly Bancroft's "metahistory" is "mythical in shape," and that shape is clearly related to what we have called the basic American myth of personal and economic freedom.

Indeed we must assume that Bancroft's history of America's political origins contributed to the development of the democratic myth in America. We must also assume, therefore, that if the democratic myth has been essentially Euro-American and if the great task before us all—Indian and white—is to enhance the role of Indian elements in the myth, then we might also assume that the scholar who undertakes a comprehensive and indeed monumental study of the vast evidence of American cultural unity may make a significant contribution to the slow process of mythogenesis which we must hope will produce in time a yet untold myth which will unite a people who so far have remained divided by their cultural differences.

WORKS CITED

Adams, Alexander. *Geronimo*. Berkley Edition. New York: Berkley, 1972.

Allen, Paula Gunn, ed. *Spiderwoman's Granddaughters*. Boston: Beacon P, 1989.

Axtell, James. *After Columbus*. New York: Oxford UP, 1988.

————. *Beyond 1492*. New York: Oxford UP, 1992.

Bradford's History of Plymouth Plantation. Ed. William T. Davis. New York: Scribner's, 1908.

Bruchac, Joseph. *Survival This Way. Interviews with American Indian Poets*.Tucson: U of Arizona P, 1987.

Costo, Rupert, and Jeannette Henry. *Textbooks and the American Indian*. San Francisco: Indian Historian P, 1970.

Costo, Rupert, and Jeannette Henry Costo, eds. *The Missions of California: A Legacy of Genocide*. San Francisco: Indian Historian P, 1987.

Daniels, John. "The Indian Population of North America in 1492." *William and Mary Quarterly*, 3rd series 49 (April 1992): 298-320.

Deloria, Vine, Jr. "Comfortable Fictions and the Struggle for Turf: An Essay Review of *The Invented Indian: Cultural Fictions and Government Policies.*" *American Indian Quarterly* 16 (Summer 1992): 397-410.

Frye, Northrop. *Fables of Identity. Studies in Poetic Mythology.* New York: Harcourt, Brace and Jovanovich, 1963.

Grinde, Donald A. "The Iroquois and the Nature of American Government." *American Indian Culture and Research Journal* 17: 1 (1993): 153-173.

Johansen, Bruce. *Forgotten Founders. How the American Indian Helped Shape Democracy.* Boston: Harvard Common P, 1982.

Kenny, Maurice. *Tekonwatonti / Molly Brant.* Fredonia, NY: White Pine P, 1992.

Smith, Donald B. *Long Lance. The True Story of an Impostor.* Lincoln: U of Nebraska P, 1982.

Zolla, Elemire. *The Writer and the Shaman. A Morphology of the American Indian.* Trans. Raymond Rosenthal. New York: Harcourt Brace Jovanovich, 1969.

THE INDIAN HISTORICAL NOVEL

ALAN VELIE, UNIVERSITY OF OKLAHOMA

A growing number of historians—most prominent among them in this country, Hayden White—is reevaluating the conception that written histories are more or less objective accounts of "what actually happened" in a given time and place.[1] Instead they are considering them more in the way that literary critics have evaluated imaginative works, examining the way histories reflect the authors' political and philosophical biases, and the way their authors shape events to conform to literary patterns. This new way of examining history is helpful in analyzing historical fiction, which always is consciously or unconsciously based on an underlying philosophy of history.

White borrows concepts from a range of thinkers from Vico to Northrop Frye in describing the way historians write history. His ideas provide a very useful schema for examining the artistic, historical and philosophical concepts underlying historical novels. Classic studies of historical fiction, works like Georg Lukács' *The Historical Novel*, are still useful as studies of writers like Scott and Manzoni, but they are naive in their conceptions of historical objectivity. Lukács was the first critic to explore in depth the different conceptions of history underlying works of fiction. He begins with Walter Scott's Waverley novels, which he contrasts with works like Flaubert's *Salammbô*, and Thackery's *Henry Esmond*. Lukács insists that Scott is "*objective*" (the italics are his) in his depiction of historical events, as opposed to Thackery, who Lucas says "dispels historical objectivity" (203). I would argue that no work of literature is objective about history, and furthermore, that no work of history is objective either. In this article I will use White's ideas to examine two recent historical novels, James Welch's *Fools Crow* and Gerald Vizenor's

---

[1] See *Metahistory*, 1, 2.

The Heirs of Columbus in terms of form, politics, and conception of history.

According to White, historical narratives are verbal models—he also uses the word "icons"—of historical events (30). The historian begins with an essentially poetic act in which he "both creates his object of analysis and predetermines the modality of the conceptual strategies he will use to explain it" (31). White describes three "levels" or "modes" the historian uses in organizing his material: emplotment, argument, and ideological implication.[2]

Before describing these terms in any detail, I should say that I am aware that they may strike the reader as arbitrary, perhaps procrustean. Too rigidly applied they would be reductive at best, and distortive at worst. However, White does not use his categories simplistically, and I will apply them less rigorously than he does. I use them chiefly to provide a vocabulary, a set of categories that is necessary in discussing any set of items. To proceed eclectically, using a variety of terms but no system, seems more confusing: e.g., referring to one historian as "Hegelian," another as "progressive," a third as "belle lettristic."

By "emplotment" White means the shape of the narrative segment. White borrows categories from Northrop Frye: romance, tragedy, comedy and satire.[3] In a romance good triumphs over evil; in satire it is the opposite: the leader fails, his country falls. Comic histories end with reconciliations between antagonists. Tragic histories end with the death of the protagonist, but not the destruction of his world.

White's categories of emplotment apply to segments of histories, series of events, as well as complete historical works. Motifs that indicate patterns of emplotment are seen in all historical narratives. Inaugural motifs include things like "Louis's troubles began when. . ." Terminating motifs include: "And so the battle of Hastings ended Saxon control of England, and brought the end of an era." Obviously the end of one era is the beginning of another, (or the middle of one conceived differently) and so an event can serve as the basis of an inaugural or terminating motif, or a transitional motif, which links the other two.

White also identifies four modes of argument: formist, organicist, mechanist,

---

[2] He also describes styles of narratives using rhetorical tropes, but since I disagree with the way he defines the tropes, I won't use that part of his scheme here.
[3] White also refers to satire as "irony." I accept Frye's categories, but prefer the term "melodrama" to "romance," and the neologism "ironedy" to "irony" which sounds more like an attitude than a form, or "satire" which parodies forms rather than being one in itself. However, in the interest of keeping down the number of terms the reader must cope with, I will use White's.

and contextualist (13ff). Formists emphasize events in their uniqueness, often focusing on the lives of national leaders. To them history is often primarily a matter of biography. Contextualists think in terms of historical trends, which imply that events are related, and periods have general tendencies. They focus on the things that make the "Gilded Age," "Progressive Era," or "Roaring Twenties" distinct from the periods that precede or follow them.

Organicists believe in patterns in history; events reflect the working of a great force, such as Hegel's World Spirit, or the inevitable progress of a nation to freedom and democracy. Mechanists are somewhat less mystical; they believe in patterns of events, but attribute them to the working out of historical laws rather than an organic force. Examples of laws would be oft repeated dicta like "the more oppressive the tyranny, the more violent the revolution," or, "people tend to revolt not when they are most downtrodden, but when their condition has begun to improve."

White chose political categories to describe Europe in the 19th Century—anarchist, radical, liberal, and conservative (22ff). These are not really suitable to Indian novels. Most Indian novels deal with the interaction of whites and Indians, and the political questions revolve around whether to be confrontational or accommodating—that is, whether to make war or peace—and whether to live separately to preserve the tribal culture, or whether to integrate into American society.

Adapting White's terms to suit the world of 19th Century Plains Indians, *Fools Crow* is a romance in terms of form, is organicist in its conception of history, and is informed by the politics of compromise.

To begin with form, readers may have trouble recognizing *Fools Crow* as a romance if they assume a novel by a plains Indian about clashes between whites and Indians in the late 19th Century would necessarily be tragic or ironic. Plains Indians did lose most of their land and much of their culture as a result of defeats at the hands of the white soldiers, but Indian writers have had a range of responses to the events.

Certainly historical works reflect the politics of their writers. For instance, most American historians, as well as popular adapters of history for Westerns, have looked on the period covered in *Fools Crow* as the "Winning of the West." Their historical and fictive accounts are generally romances, showing the settling of the West by whites and their conquest of the Indians as a good thing, a triumph of civilization.

Accounts written from an Indian point of view, like John Neihardt's *Black Elk*

Speaks, have, not surprisingly, often taken the ironic perspective: the subjugation of the Indians and their forced assimilation into American life is a great loss to the Indians, a form of spiritual extinction as a people. It is interesting to note, however, the fact that Neihardt had a bleaker view of Indian history than Black Elk himself did. Neihardt neglects to point out that Black Elk became a Christian, and evidently viewed his life in more comic terms than his biographer—comic not in the sense of humorous, but in the sense of warring cultures coming to an accommodation and blending. Neihardt ends his narrative with the massacre at Wounded Knee, and Black Elk's horrified reaction to it. Neihardt makes Black Elk's last words:

> A people's dream died there. . . . There is no center any longer, and the sacred tree is dead. (276)

Lame Deer, who also wrote a memoir of Sioux life, tells of Black Elk riding a horse with his daughter behind him reading him the Bible (216). Neihardt chooses not to include Black Elk's conversion; he chooses to make the narrative a satire in White's terms, a tale of the death of a culture.

Stanley Vestal's biography of Sitting Bull is tragic in that it ends with the death of an individual, but the survival of his people. Furthermore, the individual, Sitting Bull, is transcendent in death. Vestal ends the book:

> Sitting Bull, leader of the largest Indian nation on the continent, the strongest, boldest, most stubborn opponent of European influence, was the very heart and soul of [the] Frontier. When the true history of the New World is written, he will receive his chapter. For Sitting Bull was one of the Makers of America. (315)

Isabel Kelsay's biography of the great Mohawk leader Joseph Brant is a comedy in the sense that it ends with the merging of two cultures. Since the time of Menander, literary comedies have ended in marriage. Histories that use the comic form of emplotment end with the marriage of peoples. This does not imply an equal partnership. In a paternalistic society the female partner loses a large measure of her identity in the marriage, and that is the fate of the Indians in their absorption into the American family.

Joseph Brant died in exile from his tribal lands. Kelsay ends her book with a description of his reburial years later:

> After a while the people of the Grand River (many of whom were becoming excellent plowmen and who, with a good income from their investments, would soon

be able to do without presents, and whom almost nobody look upon as "savage")
took prideful thought of their great man who lay so many miles away. By the side
of the little, old Mohawk church they set about to prepare a proper resting place
for him. . . . And on the shoulders of strong, young grandsons of men he had
known, Joseph Thayendanegea was carried, by relays, back home. (658)

White Americans, whether sympathetic or not to Indian concerns, tend to
view Indian history in tragic or ironic terms, thinking primarily in terms of Indian
failures and disasters. Virtually all Oklahomans know about the Trail of Tears; few
are aware that Tulsa was founded by the Creeks, many of whom became successful
ranchers and businessmen. That negative orientation leads readers to assume literary works like *Fools Crow* are tragic or ironic.

In fact, the description of *Fools Crow* that appears on the book jacket describes
the novel as a tragedy.[4] Like many Americans who believe themselves sympathetic
to Indians, the blurb writer is so predisposed to see Indians as a "people with a
plight" that he or she imagines a tragic ending even though Welch didn't write one.
Although the book skirts tragedy, it ends on a positive, indeed triumphant and de-
fiant note, the hallmark of romance:

> For even though he [Fools Crow] was, like Feather Woman burdened with the
> knowledge of his people, their lives and the lives of their children, he knew they
> would survive, for they were the chosen ones. (390)

Welch is of course aware of the hardships—indeed, disasters—endured by the
Blackfeet after they were forced to abandon their traditional way of life. However,
he chooses to depict Blackfeet history in a positive rather than negative manner, as
a romance rather than satire. To anyone with a developed sense of literary form, it
ought to be apparent from the beginning that *Fools Crow* will end with the hero
triumphant. The book is a *Bildungsroman* of sorts. At the beginning the hero is a
bit older than the traditional youth; White Man's Dog, as he's called at the time, is
eighteen, but he clearly is callow and unaccomplished. Welch starts with the "poor
luckless lad" language that traditionally introduces the rags to riches motif:

> Not so lucky was White Man's Dog. He had little to show for his eighteen winters.
> His father, Rides-at-the-door, had many horses and three wives. He himself had
> three horses and no wives. His animals were puny, not a blackhorn runner among
> them. He owned a musket and no powder and his animal helper was weak. Many

[4]"Its grave and measured handling of an indelible [sic] American subject achieves
the dignity of classical tragedy" is the full quote.

times he had prayed to the Above Ones for stronger medicine but he knew that wasn't the way. It was up to him, perhaps with the help of a many-faces man, to find his own power. (3, 4)

In depicting White Man's Dog in these terms, Welch is drawing upon two traditions. One is the Blackfeet myth of Scarface, an unpromising hero who begins poor and disfigured, but becomes a hero and teaches the Blackfeet the ritual of the Sundance.[5] The other tradition is the Horatio Alger tradition of the lad who pulls himself up by his bootstraps. In understanding that Welch thinks of himself as Blackfeet and draws on Blackfeet myths and traditions, we should not forget that he grew up in America soaking in the same myths from the books, comics, films, and television shows as other Americans, Black, white or Asian.

Knowledge of either the Indian or Anglo tradition should tip off the reader that White Man's Dog is destined for great things—and sure enough, he is. He distinguishes himself in a raid against the Crows, gaining many horses. His wealth and reputation allow him to acquire a beautiful wife. He becomes a many-faces man himself, a man of great power. At the climax of the novel he undertakes a quest which teaches him why the Blackfeet are having such a difficult time. They are the people of Feather Woman, the wife of Morning Star, daughter-in-law of Sun and Moon, who transgressed a taboo and was punished by banishment. Her punishment extends to her people the Blackfeet, whose afflictions come at the hands of the Napikwans, the whites. Feather Woman tells Fools Crow that

"One day I will rejoin my husband and son. I will return with them to their lodge and there we will be happy again—and your people will suffer no more." (352)

Until that happy day Fools Crow is to prepare the Blackfeet for the times to come, and to pass down the stories of their greatness, so that their descendants know what a great people the Blackfeet were.

This is a muted sort of romance compared to more melodramatic works like *The Odyssey* or Hollywood westerns, where the good guys destroy the bad guys, but it is a romance nonetheless. Welch has a choice to end his novel with the Blackfeet being massacred by the Cavalry, an event he describes (378), or with the decimation of the Blackfeet by smallpox, which he also describes (371). He could have concluded the novel with the total demoralization of his people, or with their pride

---

[5] Nora Berry develops the parallels between Scarface and White Man's Dog at length in "A Myth to be Alive": James Welch's *Fools Crow*.

in surviving. He chooses to end it on a note of pride:

> That night there was much feasting in all the Pikuni camps. Winter was over and the men talked of hunting, of moving the camps out of the valleys, of moving on. The women prepared their meager feast and fed their men, their children, their relatives and friends. They knew that soon the meat pots would be full and the hides would be drying in the sun. Outside, the children played in the rain, chasing each other, slipping and skidding in the mud. They were Pikunis and they played hard. (390)

This is not the language of tragedy or satire; it is the language of romance.

Welch's depiction of history in *Fools Crow* as the result of the action of the gods is organicist in conception. That is, historical events are related as what White terms "components of synthetic processes" (15). Hegel, who saw history as the "rationally necessary course of the World Spirit" (12), and "the working of Providence"(82), is perhaps the most explicit of post Enlightenment historians in his organicist beliefs. Leading romantic American historians of the nineteenth century, men like Bancroft, Prescott, Motley and Parkman, were less mystical in their language, but they share with Hegel the notion that history "was the unfolding of a vast Providential plan" (Levin 26).

The philosophy that underlies *Fools Crow* is similar to that of Parkman *et al* in that human events reflect divine intentions, but Blackfeet polytheism causes an important difference. To Hegel and American romantics the course of human history might not have always run smoothly from the perspective of individual men or peoples, but an omnipotent, omnibenevolent God was in control. The problem of the Blackfeet was that their tutelary diety, Feather Woman, had sinned against more powerful gods, and the tribe was being punished with her. Ultimately, however, she will be restored to grace, and the tribe with her.

The politics of *Fools Crow* might best be described as accommodational. Welch presents a number of viewpoints in the novel, but the most responsible and sympathetic leaders advocate compromising with the whites, chiefly on pragmatic grounds.

The most aggressive attitude is that of the renegades, Fast Horse, Owl Child and their band, Indians who had broken with the Blackfeet, and who harried white settlers, killing them, burning their homes, and stealing their horses. Owl Child's reaction to the encroachment of the whites and their herds of cattle is to kill as many of the *Napikwans* as possible before they can establish a foothold. "Some day, old man," he says to Three Bears,

"a Napikwan will be standing right where you are and all around him will be graz-
ing thousands of the whitehorns. You will be only part of the dust they kick up. If
I have my way I will kill that white man and all his whitehorns before this happens...We will show you what real Pikunis do to these sonofabitch whites." (61)

What Owl Child says is consonant with the Blackfeet code of death before dis-
honor, and warfare as the proper way of settling foreign policy disputes. Although
some romantic idealists among contemporary Americans like to think of Indians
as sylvan pacifists, this is not, nor has ever been, the view Plains Indians held of
themselves. As Vine Deloria points out in *Custer Died for Your Sins*,

The Sioux, my own people, have a great tradition of conflict. We were the only nation ever to annihilate the United States Cavalry three times in succession. And
when we have no one else to quarrel with, we often fight each other. . . .During
one twenty-year period in the last century the Sioux fought over an area from La-
Crosse, Wisconsin, to Sheridan, Wyoming against the Crow, Arapaho, Cheyenne,
Mandan, Arikara, Hidatsa, Ponca, Iowa, Pawnee, Otoe, Omaha, Winnebago,
Chippewa, Cree, Assiniboine, Sac and Fox, Potowatomi, Ute, and Gros Ventre.
(29)

In *Fools Crow* Welch mentions battles between the Blackfeet, who pride themselves on being the scourge of the northern plains, and the Cree, Gros Ventre, and
Crows. But those spokesmen in the novel who represent Welch's position (or the
"implied" Welch, to use the formalist distinction) have a sense of *Realpolitik*: they
realize that the whites are far too numerous, well armed, and technologically advanced to defeat. The logistical problems are impossible. The Indians have no
source to resupply arms and ammunition other than what they can capture, and
they must travel with their women and children, while the families of the Cavalry
are out of reach of Indian attack. Accordingly, the voices of moderation counsel ne-
gotiation with the whites, preferably from a position of strength—that is, before it
is too late, while they still control valuable land. Rides-at-the-Door argues:

The great war between the Napikiwans far to the east [the Civil War] is over. More
and more of the seizers who fought for Ka-ach-sino, the great grandfather, have
moved out to our country. More will still come. If we take the war road against the
whites, we will sooner or later encounter great numbers of them. Even with many-
shots guns we couldn't hope to match their weapons . . . .And so we must fend for
ourselves, for our survival. That is why we must treat with the Napikwans. (177)

There is also an extreme position of accommodation, one that Welch seems to
find as distasteful as extreme aggressiveness. White Man Dog reasons:

His father was right and wise to attempt to treat with the Napikwans. But one day these blue-coated warriors would come, and White Man's Dog and the other young men would be forced to fight to the death. It would be better to die than to end up standing around the fort, waiting for handouts that never came. Some bands, like the Grease Melters, had already begun to depend too much on the Napikwans. Ever since the Big Treaty they journeyed to the agent's house for the commodities that were promised to them. Most of the time they returned empty-handed. (93)

The politics of *Fools Crow* are clear: the Blackfeet must negotiate with the whites, but they must do it from a position of strength. To fight for a prolonged period would mean extermination for the tribe. To give in without driving a hard bargain would lead to starvation and humiliation. Welch is well aware that the Blackfeet did lose many people to starvation one winter shortly after the period covered in *Fools Crow*. He has written about that ordeal elsewhere.[6] Nonetheless, the values of the Fools Crow are clear: the Blackfeet must cut the best bargain they can; they owe it to their children. The tribe must survive. Ultimately history will be on their side—Feather Woman will be returned to grace, and so will they.

Fools Crow is a familiar looking historical novel, more or less similar to Scott's Waverley novels. Like Scott, Welch writes about a romantic people whose wild, free way of life is over but not forgotten. In fact, the Blackfeet, like the Scots, are a war-like people who love nature, have little use for material possessions, live in the wilds, and are crushed and civilized by the less courageous but more numerous Anglo Saxons. Like the Blackfeet the Scots were tribal—*gentile* is the phrase Lukács uses—clans being the chief social unit (57). The appeal of the traditional historical novel is that it makes the reader long nostalgically for a way of life that has been destroyed.

In *The Heirs of Columbus*, Gerald Vizenor has written a very different type of historical novel, a postmodern version of the genre in which he abandons verisimilitude for absurdist fantasy. This may seem "unhistorical" to those who expect historical fiction to look like a Waverley novel, but Vizenor is just as interested in historical questions as Scott or Welch; he merely uses a different set of conventions to consider them.[7]

In fact, *Heirs* is only partially a historical novel: the sections on Columbus,

---

[6] Viz. the ordeal of the hero 's grandmother in *Winter in the Blood*. Welch says that he is planning a novel on the subject.

[7] For what it's worth, Scott doesn't seem all that verisimilar to me, despite what Lukács and other apologists say.

Pocahantas, and Louis Riel are based on history, but much of the novel fits more closely the conventions of other genres, in particular the murder mystery and utopian science fiction tale. However, Vizenor's ideas of history when contrasted with those of more traditional historical writers like Welch, serve to point up the literary nature of all historical writing.

In form *Heirs* is a romance, although the tone and conventions are those of comedy. To be more specific, it is a parody of a romance, even though it has a serious theme. Parodies of melodramas or romances—e.g., novels like Graham Greene's *Our Man in Havana* or Evelyn Waugh's *Scoop*, or films like *Airplane* or *Naked Gun 2 1/2*—utilize the form of romance, the plot structure pitting a group of heroes against villains, good guys aginst bad guys, culminating in a showdown, while retaining the conventions of comedy, the humorous tone and outlandish events.

In *Heirs* the heroes are Christopher Columbus and his Indian descendants, Anishinaabe from the White Earth Reservation in Minnesota, and their fellow tribesmen and allies. Columbus generated a good deal of interest among Indians as well as whites in his quincentenary year, and since negative treatments of Columbus by Indians have received a good deal of attention, it may be surprising to find that Vizenor makes Columbus not only sympathetic, but Indian.

Stone Columbus, descendant of the explorer, and radio talk show host, explains that "Columbus was Mayan. . ."

> "The Maya brought civilization to the savages of the OldWorld and the rest is natural," said Stone. "Columbus escaped from the culture of death and carried our tribal genes back to the New World, back to the great river, he was an adventurer in our blood and he returned to his homeland." (9)

This may seem preposterous in a historical novel, but actually it is not much more farfetched than what the reader is asked to swallow about Ivanhoe and his adventures with the Jewish Rebecca on the one hand or the mythical Robin Hood on the other. The main difference between *Ivanhoe* and *Heirs* is that Scott labors to retain what Henry James called "an air of reality" (14), even in Sherwood Forest, while Vizenor opts for the conventions of comedy, both tribal and western, which flout verisimilitude.

Samuel Eliot Morison, in his biography of Columbus, ridicules the claims earlier writers had made about the explorer's nationality—he was Portuguese, French, English, Greek, etc.—and adds what he considers the most preposterous hypothesis of all: "It only remains for some American patrioteer to come forward and claim that Columbus was really an Indian. . ."(6).

Vizenor is that "patrioteer," but his motive is hardly American chauvinism; rather he wishes to refigure Columbus for Indians, to defang the monster who enslaved Indians, and opened the door to their slaughter and subjugation. A major purpose of the novel, as Vizenor explains in the epilogue, is the domestication of Columbus, reclaiming him for Indians and rendering him harmless:

> Columbus arises in tribal stories that heal with humor the world he wounded; he is loathed, but he is not a separation in tribal conciousness. The Admiral of the Ocean Sea is a trickster overturned in his own stories five centuries later. (185)

The larger goal of *Heirs* is to depict a utopia in which the genes of the survivor Columbus could be used to heal the rifts between Indian and Indian (mixedblood and fullblood, tribal leaders and ordinary members) and Indian and white.

Columbus becomes Indian when his Indian lover, Samana, liberates the stories in his blood that had been passed down to him from his mother.

> He inherited the signature of survivance and tribal stories in the blood from his mother, and she inherited the genetic signature from maternal ancestors. (28)

Samana liberates Columbus's soul, and the stories in his blood, through sex:

> Samana dove from the sterncastle into the shadows at the mouth of the river... Columbus removed his scarlet tunic and followed her in the water. That night he abandoned the curve of his pain in her hands and thighs and entered her maw to become a woman, a bear, a hand talker. . . . Overnight his discoveries reduced tribal cultures to the status of slaves; at the same time the stories in his blood were liberated by a tribal hand talker. (40, 41)

In retelling the story of Columbus in order to gain control over it for tribal people, Vizenor's methods and conventions are very different from those of a historical novelist like Scott, or a historian like Morison, but we must remember that Scott and Morison also shape events to fit literary patterns and political and philosophical preconceptions. Historians vigorously protest that they are objective and bound by the truth, nonetheless it is historians who have made the claim that Columbus was French, Greek or German—not to mention that Shakespeare was Bacon or that slaves in the ante-bellum South were better off than Northern workers.

These historians would argue that their claims are based on objective historical evidence. Vizenor is more phenomenological; he advances the Indian belief that the world exists in the imagination: "The New World is heard, the tribal world is dreamed and imagined"(93) he puts it in one place; "some tribal people would say that the real world exists and is remembered nowhere else but in stories" (75), is the way he states it in another.

Samana makes her way to the headlands of the Mississippi River, and passes Columbus's "genetic signature" and the "stories in his blood" to his heirs, one of whom, Stone Columbus, is the protagonist of the book. Stone is a radio talk show host who helps found a utopian tribal colony called Point Assinka on Point Roberts in Puget Sound. The heirs of Columbus (others are Truman Columbus, Stone's grandmother, and Binn, his mother) declare Point Assinka a free state with "no prisons, no passports, no public schools, no missionaries, no television, and no public taxation. . ."

The colony finances itself through bingo, using the funds it generates to fund cures for wounded, deformed, and lonesome people. The cures are affected through genetic surgery. The process, "electrophoresis," involves radioactive genetic mutation, infusing the genes of the patients with the "genetic code of tribal survivance and radiance" (133), handed down through 5000 generations to Columbus, and so to his heirs.

The mystery in the novel revolves around the remains of Columbus and Pocahantas. One of the villains, Doric Miched, has acquired the casket that holds what is left of Columbus. Felipa Flowers, a "poacher" who liberates Indian artifacts from whites who have illicitly acquired them, uses shamanic magic to get the explorer's remains. She then tries to get the remains of Pocahantas, but is killed by Miched in the attempt. At the climax of the novel, Columbus, Pocahantas and Felipa are all buried on Point Assinka. Miched is never convicted of the murder, but is imprisoned for other crimes.

The other villain, the *wiindigoo*, or Evil Gambler, is adapted from Anishinaabe folklore. Vizenor depicts him as a blond water demon with a perfect smile who gambles with tribal members for their lives. Ice Woman freezes him solid, but he is thawed by "federal operatives" to punish the heirs. At the end of the book, the *wiindigoo* takes on the heirs in gambling game. If he wins the world will be destroyed. The *wiindigoo* loses his nerve, and instead of taking his turn, fades into the shadows. It is the showdown typical of romance; goodness prevails, evil is controlled.

Vizenor's political ideas may seem different from Welch's in that *Fool's Crow* ends with the Blackfeet living among whites in Montana, while *Heirs* ends with Vizenor's vision of a utopian separatist community. But both Vizenor and Welch are pragmatists who steer a middle course between confrontation and submission, advocating tribal basis of Indian life, and driving the best bargain one can with the whites that circumstances allow. *Fools Crow* is set in the past; Welch endorses the course the Blackfeet actually took. *Heirs* ends with a futurist fantasy which explores what might happen if tribal sovereignty were extended and bingo revenue greatly increased.

In his nonfiction works Vizenor makes it clear he avoids the extremes of the confrontational policies of AIM, which he detests and has fought for years,[8] and the collusional corruption of tribal officials who get rich by playing footsie with white developers (*Crossbloods* xxvi).

Vizenor also takes the middle ground between right and left in white America when they argue about Indian matters. In *Crossbloods* he ridicules Ronald Reagan, who said:

> "Maybe we made a mistake in trying to maintain Indian cultures. Maybe we should not have humored them in wanting to stay in that kind of primitive lifestyle." (xxiii)

On the left Vizenor pillories the politically correct "romantics and culture cultists" who have

> homogenized tribal philosophies and transvalued tribal visions into counterculture slogans and environmental politics. (16)

For Vizenor, as for Welch, the most important aspect of Indian rights is tribal sovereignty.

Vizenor's political ideas are tied closely to his aesthetic ideas, which derive from Anishinaabe literature, particularly trickster tales. Vizenor's creed is stated in his first novel, *Darkness in Saint Louis Bearheart.* Third Proude Cedarfair, a "warrior diplomat," says:

> "Outwit but never kill evil. . .The tricksters and warriorclowns have stopped more evil violence with their wit than have lovers with their lust and fools with their power and rage. . ." (11)

---

[8] See, for instance, *Crossbloods* iii-xvi, 188-192, 299.

Tricksters battle evil with wit and humor. The trickster is essentially comic; "a comic trope," "comic nature in a language game," is the way Vizenor puts it in *The Trickster of Liberty* (x). Comedy is communal; tragedy works in isolating the hero, separating him from his people. Comedy seals separations between people and peoples. The storyteller sends the trickster forth into the world to heal its rifts:

> The trickster is immortal; when the trickster emerges in imagination the author dies in comic discourse. To imagine the tribal trickster is to relume human unities; colonial surveillance, monologues, and racial separations are overturned in discourse. (x)

Vizenor combats evil through stories, comic stories like the trickster tales that were common to all Indian tribes. As Memphis the panther says in *Heirs*, these stories have "power to heal," (71) and the power to heal is comic.[9]

In his fantasy Vizenor deals with a number of serious political issues for Indians: tribal sovereignty, ownership of tribal artifacts and human remains, and Indian gambling. With the flourishing of Indian gambling in recent years—bingo now generates millions of dollars annually for tribes, and casino gambling, with potentially higher revenues is just beginning—legal questions have arisen concerning the rights of tribes to be considered sovereign nations, outside the scope of state and federal laws. The United States government granted tribes sovereign status during the 18th and 19th centuries, withholding some of the prerogatives of citizenship. Today with tribal members holding full American citizenship, the legal questions are complex, and have not been fully ajudicated. Vizenor's utopia at Point Assinka—a tax-free sovereign country, financed by bingo—may seem fanciful, but it is merely an extension of the situation that could easily occur under current law on any reservation in the U.S. Many people, including Vizenor, worry about poor people squandering rent money, or becoming addicted to gambling, or even that the Mafia will take over bingo operations, but despite these dangers, Vizenor sees bingo as a boon for the Indian community, which has had little money coming in over the years.[10] And, as Vizenor points out in his depiction of the *wiindigoo*, gambling is a very old tradition among Indians.

The status and ownership of Indian artifacts and remains is also a serious topic of this humorous novel. Anthropologists have acquired, by theft, purchase, or

---

[9] The power of stories is a common theme in Indian literature. Viz. Vizenor's *Dead Voices*, Leslie Silko's *Ceremony*, and Scott Momaday's *Ancient Child*.
[10] For a discussion of Indian bingo, see *Crossbloods* 18-24.

grave robbery, Indian remains and sacred objects, and kept them or delivered them to museums. Tribes have tried to regain the bodies and possessions of their ancestors, but have often been balked in the courts.[11]

The incident in which Felipa Flowers dies while trying to "liberate" the bones of Pocahantas may seem fantastic, but the issue is serious. In *Crossbloods* Vizenor tells the story of a bulldozer operator in Iowa who dug up an unmarked cemetery, unearthing the remains of twenty-seven people. Twenty-six were reburied, but because of beads found with the remains of the twenty-seventh the state archeologist demanded that the bones be sent to him under state law. He got them (69).

Vizenor shares Welch's organicist conception of history, though Vizenor's supernatural forces are less anthropomorphic. In the case of *Fools Crow* Blackfeet deities influence the course of history. In *Heirs* there is no mention of a deity with a providential plan; history is working out of stories in the blood, stories passed from one people to another, from the Jews to the Mayas, descendants of the Lost Tribe of Israel,[12] to Columbus and his heirs among the Anishinaabe. Columbus first sensed the stories when he met Sephardic Jews in Europe before his voyage to the New World. Samana lured him to San Salvador with the idea of liberating the stories in his blood.

To Vizenor, stories are the way cultures come to terms with existence, how they make sense of the world around them. But stories are not simply produced consciously or unconciously by societies; they belong to the realm of nature as much as culture. Vizenor extends Jung's ideas about narrative structures and archetypes being transmitted from one generation to the next; he describes how stories are actually transmitted from one generation to the next genetically.

> "The genome narratives are stories in the blood, a metaphor for racial memories, or the idea that we inherit the structures of language and genetic memories. . ." (136)

says Pir Cantrip, leading genetic researcher at Point Assinka.

Stories in the blood are linked to what Vizenor terms the "genes of survivance," a set of superior genes passed down from the ancient Mayans through Columbus to his heirs (170). The stories in the blood and the genes of survivance were

---

[11] See *Crossbloods* 62-82.
[12] That Indians are descendants of the Lost Tribe of Israel is a belief of a number of tribes, as well as the Mormons. The Cherokees have a myth that they are descended from "Zega," Ezekiel.

the "new moities to heal" and Point Assinka "the first crossblood nation dedicated to heal the wounded with genetic therapies"(144).

Since people are using genetic therapy to influence the course of history, this is a very different conception from most types of organicism, which posit some form of Providence as the controlling force behind history. However, the way Vizenor describes it, the genes seem to have their own agenda, and Cantrip and the other therapists are really following the mandate of the genes. In some ways Vizenor's ideas seem reminiscent of those of sociobiologist Edward Wilson, who argues that

> in a Darwinist sense the organism does not live for itself. Its primary function is not even to reproduce other organisms; it reproduces genes, and it serves as their temporary carrier. (3)

In conclusion, James Welch and Gerald Vizenor have written novels that appear to be radically different. Both however are historical novels, novels which not only describe historical events, but shape them in accordance with narrative, political and historical concepts. In being aware of how Indian authors shape history when describing it, we can learn not only about the Indians of yesterday, but also of today.

WORKS CITED

Barry, Norma. "A Myth to Be Alive." MELUS 17,1 (Spring 1991-2): 3-20.

Deloria, Vine Jr. *Custer Died For Your Sins*. New York: Avon, 1969.

Hegel, Georg. *Reason in History*. New York: Library of Liberal Arts, 1953.

James, Henry. *The Future of the Novel*. New York: Random House, 1956.

Kelsay, Isabel Thompson. *Joseph Brant*. Syracuse: Syracuse UP, 1984.

Lame Deer, John (Fire). *Lame Deer Seeker of Visions*. New York: Simon and Schuster, 1972.

Lukács, Georg. *The Historical Novel*. Lincoln: U of Nebraska P, 1983.

Neihardt, John G. *Black Elk Speaks*. Lincoln: U of Nebraska P, 1961.

Vestal, Stanley. *Sitting Bull, Champion of the Sioux*. Boston: Houghton Mifflin, 1932.

Vizenor, Gerald. *Crossbloods*. Minneapolis: U of Minnesota Press, 1990.

___. *The Heirs of Columbus*. Hanover: UP of New England, 1991.

Welch, James. *Fools Crow*. New York: Viking, 1986.

White, Hayden. *Metahistory*. Baltimore: Johns Hopkins UP, 1973.

Wilson, Edward O. *Sociobiology* (the abridged edition), Cambridge: Harvard UP, 1980.

Boxcar Babies:
The Santa Fe Railroad Indian Village at Richmond, California, 1940-1945

KURT M. PETERS, UNIVERSITY OF CALIFORNIA, BERKELEY

When my father returned from World War Two weekends became filled with discovery of the midwestern countryside. Similar to many post-war families, ours was mandated with assisting the returnee in locating a sense of belonging in non-military society. For the previous five years I had remained with my mother in the warmth of my maternal grandparent's home, insulated from and only vaguely frightened by the radio reports of the War's destruction of faraway villages and cities. Now we three became weekend nomads, touring the back roads of middle America in our second-hand family automobile. My father drove us no place in particular on Sundays, although a pattern of returning to sites that had occupied my parent's time prior to the War seemed to emerge.

What is most memorable for me about this era, however, is the appearance of emergency housing for some of the returning veterans. I suppose that many, like my father, came straight from the battlefields to the relative stability of a home place, there to have their ravaged psyches jerk and lurch their way back into the institutionalized norms of American life. Others were not as fortunate, or so it seemed. This possibility was reflected in some of the returnee's housing that we observed on our outings.

Many veterans found that wartime had created a dearth of materials, with a concurrent lack of construction and limited labor for non-military ventures. Production of all types conformed to a military focus in the 1940's, and post-war change along the dusty agrarian byways had not yet begun in 1946. At the War's end there was simply not enough residential housing to satisfy the immediate needs of budding American families: many occupied any structure that could provide minimal protection from the elements.

Our weekend excursions to the rural areas often brought us the sight of whole families peering from chicken coops and other small nondescript buildings converted to housing. Their homes were no more than elemental shacks, tar paper and a few boards, with no visible amenities and little protection from adversity. The people near the dwellings returned our stares as we drove on: tourists from just a few miles away viewing gawkers from another world. There always seemed to be a barren, hopeless pall over the scenes passing by, and whatever commenting my parents did about the "pitiful state" of these post-war families was not lost on me. I turned the vignettes over and over in my imagination. I dangled the visions in the center of my child's smug assuredness, considered them, and decided that indeed my parent's judgmental analysis was correct.

In truth, none of us riding by knew anything of the lives of these people, how they actually came to be there, or what circumstances held them in that place. They were little more than pasteboard cutouts in a distant stage scene on which I passed my critical review. What I didn't understand at the time was that the distance between us and the people outside their shacks was not an enormous abyss, but rather only a fine line drawn by familial ties and economic circumstance. There was also the slight possibility of choice on the part of the inhabitants of the shacks.

I since have wondered what life for those families must have been, when and where they found their hope for the future, and what ties knotted together the shreds of their collective sense of being. The answer to all this is beyond revelation: the moment for validation of their stories has long passed. My questioning came at a time when I could not, would not, have been allowed to explicitly investigate such matters. Experiences of intervening years have ground down the sharp edges of those impressions. Today, such visions would not startle me as they did then but would certainly titillate my interest for asking "why," and "what," and so on.

That original collage of sadness and curiosity, and my long ago reactions, were recalled while reading the oral testimony of Marguerite Williams, a lifetime resident of the San Francisco Bay area. The narrator, descended from a Louisiana slave family, remembered Native American workers coming to Richmond, California, as wartime employees of the Santa Fe Railroad. The families were living in the railroad yards in housing provided by the Company, and their children attended the local elementary school. She found the Indians to be "shy," and learned that they "didn't mingle." However, befriending several through the school's Parent Teacher Association, an opportunity eventually came to visit the home of one Indian family. Her reactions to the living conditions in the train yards are related during an interview with the University of California's Judith K. Dunning:

> Dunning: What can you tell me about the Indian Village?
> M. Williams: There was just kind of a little enclave over there. What it was, the Santa Fe, they hired a lot of the Indians from New Mexico, and they gave them housing.
> But what you call housing, oh my goodness, they were just pitiful. It was really pathetic. I just said that it was terrible that a big industry like Santa Fe would put those people in those little hovels.
> Dunning: Were they wooden?
> M. Williams: Yes. They were wood, little wooden shacks. They wouldn't have to worry too much about heat because they were so small.
> Dunning: How large a community was it out there?
> M. Williams: They had about fifteen families. Each one of them, they had these little bitty houses. The only way they would get relief was if one of the girls would get married. Other than that, they would have about six or seven kids, so eight people were living in one little shack.
> Dunning: When did this start?
> M. Williams: I don't know. (113)

Between 1900 and 1945 thousands of people migrated to the San Francisco Bay area, principally as laborers for the expanding empires of the automotive, railroad and shipbuilding industries. As a result of these movements the region near Richmond, California, along the Bay north of Oakland, became heavily infused with migrant workers. One such group of people came from the Laguna Pueblo in New Mexico as employees of the Santa Fe Railroad, first arriving at Richmond in 1922.

The operations of the Santa Fe Railroad were being crippled by a national strike (*Labor Conflict*). A substantial number of Lagunas met the railroad's needs, based on an oral agreement made with the railroad by their tribe in 1880, and migrated to the Richmond Terminal to bolster a depleted work force.[1] During their lengthy sojourn a set of boxcars, completely enclosed by the railroad yards, eventually constituted their housing. Nonetheless, within this enclave, they continued traditional cultural practices, forming a microcosmic extension of their distant pueblo.

---

[1] According to interviews with Laguna descendants of the men in this "First Group," the total was about 100; Santiago B. and Nellie A. Sarracino, taped and personal interviews; University of California, Berkeley and Laguna Pueblo, New Mexico, September 1991-May 1993, Ruth Hopper, personal interviews; University of California, Berkeley, September 1991-May 1993, and others. Hereinafter referred to as "Personal interviews."

Subsequent waves of migrant Lagunas, buttressed with members of the Acoma Pueblo from New Mexico, passed in and out of the terminal at Richmond between 1922 and the mid-1980's, when the "Indian Village," as it had become known, was finally disbanded. They adapted themselves to the surrounding non-Indian functions but clung to tradition, returning often to the Pueblo for nurturing celebrations and rituals. Children were born in the Village, later referring to themselves as "boxcar babies," while others migrated from Laguna with their parents. Scores of Lagunas were raised in the Village and educated nearby. At one point over twenty Laguna children attended the local elementary school. Some of the Catholic Village residents participated in masses celebrated at Our Lady of Mercy Catholic Church, at nearby Point Richmond. Tribal members working for Santa Fe demonstrated knowledge of the value of their skills, joining railroad craft unions when the work force at large voted to organize.

Notably, however, during the workers' employment at Richmond the Village functioned as a de facto satellite of the distant Laguna Pueblo. Sociologically and psychologically the Village remained inextricably a part of the home Pueblo, much as if it were situated nearby, along the railroad right-of-way, west of the Rio Grande River in New Mexico. The shared experience of those who intermittently occupied the Village is at once a tribute to cultural persistence and pragmatic accommodation by those who participated in honoring the oral contract with Santa Fe. In the process the participants not only extended the vitality of the Laguna Pueblo community but expanded significantly their people's rich cultural tradition.

James Gregory, in a history of migration to the Bay Area, describes Richmond as a "dull industrial suburb" with a population of about 24,000 residents in 1940 (176). The Santa Fe shops at Richmond employed increasing numbers of the Railroad's work force, which grew as trackage increased and the southwestern lands became more settled. A second group of Lagunas came to live in the terminal yards, sometime in the late 1930's. This time more permanent housing was being provided by the Company, in the form of remodeled boxcars set in rows on sidings. One of the wartime laborers who lived more than thirty years in the boxcar "Indian Village" tells of his employment experience:

A. "Yeah, I was just one of the kids (on) the reservation. I was twenty-two when I went out there to work Santa Fe.

"I start from labor. Then they asked me if I want to be a coach cleaner. Yeah, I said, so they put me on. Then they asked me if I want to be (an electrician's job was offered).

"I got that job and after that, I learned my job, you know. Had a good electrician teach me and did pretty good. I learned from him how to fix air conditioning motors, all kinds of lights, you know." (Personal interviews)

The total Santa Fe work force grew from 41,300 in 1940 to 53,890 in 1943 as World War Two production expanded (Waters, 325). The introduction of the Kaiser Shipyards to meet wartime needs, added to the Santa Fe Shops, Standard Oil Refinery and the Ford assembly plant, brought Richmond the distinction of being the "quintessential war boom town" and a population exceeding 100,000 in three years of rapid growth (Gregory 176).[2]

As the Santa Fe system grew after 1940, the migration of Native Americans to points of employment along the railway continued. Major concentrations of Indian labor occurred at the growing junctures of the railroad and urban populations. By World War Two there were six historic Villages at the Laguna Reservation and four new settlements elsewhere, along the lines of the Santa Fe. The outlying groups are often reported by scholars as "colonies" of Old Laguna (Spicer, *Cycles* 554; Rands 272). The noted anthropologist, Edward Spicer, considered these colonies to be "wholly dependent on the general economy," but bonded to the homeland as "extensions of the reservation communities" (*Cycles*, 554).

A daughter of Lagunas living at the Richmond Village during the War years recalls that her father came with the "second group" of men, and her mother later. Initially, her father was bunked in the Santa Fe's firehouse, but when the family arrived, housing in the boxcars was utilized. Her mother describes the influx of migrating Laguna families and their living arrangements, just prior to the Second World War:

Q. "Do you remember the housing?"
A. 'Well the houses were set up...at first they were boxcars sitting on the railroad tracks. And each family had a house, a boxcar, you know, a regular boxcar.
"They kind of made it look like, what do you call those darn things, mobile homes?
"The railroad had decided to set up homes for the Laguna people."
Q. "Regular homes, you mean?"
A. "Yeah, they built regular homes. Well, they were boxcars, but made into duplexes (later they added) a kitchen and the bathroom." (Personal interviews)

When Lewis Meriam toured the habitat of Native Americans during 1927-

---

2 See also Scott, Mel.

1928, he was directing an investigative project for the Institute For Government Research, at the request of Hubert Work, the Secretary of the Interior. The result would be the now classic *Problem of Indian Administration*, which devotes dozens of its pages to the social, health, and employment conditions of so-called "Industrially Housed Indians."

While investigating the southwest, his project team surveyed conditions of Native American workers in major cities in New Mexico, Arizona, and California. The Santa Fe yards at Richmond were apparently bypassed, possibly since the major growth in the population of Pueblo workers there didn't occur until well after 1935. His description of the laborer's boxcar houses in other areas visited gives insight to this phenomenon at Richmond, however:

> Living Conditions. To house the Indians the railroad company placed rows of box cars within the roundhouse yard at each city. A partition divides each car into two rooms. At Winslow (Arizona) the railroad company has forty-three cars in a colony near the round-house. Nineteen cars are occupied by one family, twenty by two families, and four by single men. At Gallup (New Mexico) twenty-three box cars are occupied by twenty-eight families, numbering ninety persons in all. Here a whole car, or two rooms, is in the majority of cases occupied by a single family. (700)

A former forty-year resident of the Richmond Village remembers that their homes were two boxcars connected in the middle by a passageway constructed to form the cars in an "H" shape. This arrangement was intended to accommodate two families, one in each boxcar. The passageways held the kitchens, which used wood burning stoves for both cooking and heat. All-wood interiors became a part of the evolution of the boxcars as living quarters, and are remembered fondly by the residents (Personal interviews). Early arrangements had the sanitary facilities located in the train yard, but eventually the Company had each boxcar "duplex" fitted with a shower and commode, one for each family.

> Q. "When the Village was first set up, did they have water inside?"
> A. "No, they had two boxcars that were set up for washrooms. One boxcar had showers, and then the other boxcar had washbowls and commodes.
> "There were three rows of boxcars and the middle set was washrooms. There was one for the ladies and then one for the men themselves, a men's washroom and a ladies washroom." (Personal interviews)

The Meriam Report summarizes the 1928 survey with the observation that domestic and waste water were hauled by the families "no more than five hundred feet," and that hot water in the communal bath and laundry houses was "always available." Each family, according to Meriam, also received free scrap wood for heat, cooking, and to fire the "several large community ovens" located near the homes. Other than a community hall, the report states that the railroad company engaged in "No other welfare work." It does comment on, however, the nature of the Santa Fe employees being observed:

> "Pueblos...belong to a culture far less primitive than that of...Indians from the large reservations. Even more important, however, is the fact that...the men are getting good pay in steady jobs which most of them have held for years. The economic status of the families is such that ...these women have the means to be, as they are even in their limited quarters, good home makers." (700-701)

"Unquestionably a box car of one or two rooms is inadequate for a family of any size," the survey notes. Meriam concludes: "If the Indians...are ever provided with more spacious and sanitary quarters, unquestionably they can and will develop their standards of housekeeping to compare favorably with the standards maintained among the wage earners of the white race" (701). Laguna families had brought to the Santa Fe Villages the values and standards of their home Pueblo. It was not apparent to the Meriam staff that the people observed enjoyed a lifestyle that met their needs as Lagunas, rather than as laborers for the railroad. The assimilationist bent of Meriam's report, by necessity or political expediency, ignored that fact and measured the quality of Laguna life by standards of non-Indians. The wife of a former head man of the Richmond Indian Village defines the need for nurturing by outsiders from the Laguna viewpoint:

> Q. "Did you use any of the services or the facilities in Richmond? Did you have what you needed?"
> A. "Oh, yeah. We had our own recreation hall where our own Indian people put up dances that could not be seen by the white people."
> Q. "So you were able to keep your own ways right there?"
> A. "Right." (Personal interviews)

Her daughter continues, explaining that the traditional Feast Days were celebrated, just as at the home pueblo, as well as social dances. Both were open to friends as they would have been if held on the reservation in New Mexico. She emphasizes her mother's earlier comment that Laguna sacred dances were also held in the Santa Fe yards, but were closed to viewing "by white people." The full round of nurturing ceremonials for maintenance of Laguna life was thereby replicated in the Richmond yards.

Railroad historian James H. Ducker noted that the practice of the Company, as early as 1886, was to grant free travel passes to "faithful employees" and their families (47). To complete the sense of maintaining ritual and personal responsibilities at home, Lagunas utilized the pass privilege for travel to and from the reservation. In addition to ceremonies, the Laguna employees of Santa Fe created an atmosphere in the boxcar village that possessed many elements of their community life in New Mexico:

> Q. "As far as things like medical, food, and all that, did you grow anything there?"
> A. "Oh, yeah, people had gardens (husband talking in background). He said that we had our own gardens, we had fruit trees...that produced fruit (laughing).
> As for the medical, the Santa Fe took care of the employees, of course. But just in case if somebody had to have surgery, or whatever, it was Santa Fe that paid for all the medical bills."

The speaker's husband joins the interview:

> Q. "I heard you had a band."
> A. "Yeah, I had an orchestra."
> Q. "Did the band go around or was it just there for the Village?"
> A. "Just for the Village. Of course, a lot of service (men) were coming in from overseas and different places so they have a nice time."
> Q. "Did any of the (military) people coming through visit out at the Village?"
> A. "Yeah, they bring some of their friends, you, know, white people. Boys, you know. Then our wives and whoever they got like a club. Fix the food, Indian food, for these service boys." (Personal interviews)

One former wartime resident, a migrant to the Village at an early age, recalls that the boxcars were pressed into many uses: as a community hall, for church confirmation dinners, traditional feasts, tribal meetings, and that one housed a "teen club" in an eight-by-ten foot room. For her, life in the Santa Fe yards was full and rich. She remembers the Village band, with an accordion, trumpet, banjo, drums, and guitar, playing music in "a style that only southwestern people know," a Spanish style of music. She relates that at a time during the war years when Black residents were not allowed in parts of Richmond after dark, credit and other favoritism was extended to the Laguna families by city merchants. Her energetic summary is that "We had everything" (Personal interviews).

According to Russell Thornton's studies of Native American migrations in the twentieth century, Indians "migrate to urban areas for economic reasons," based on perhaps ill-conceived notions that "good job opportunities" await them (230). The foundation for the movement of Lagunas along the westward expansion of the Santa Fe lines was built on other than speculative employment possibilities, however. It was the motivating power of a specialized agreement with the Santa Fe Railroad, coupled with a changing economic structure at Old Laguna, that caused Lagunas to migrate to the San Francisco Bay area.

Land tenure conflicts in New Mexico had plagued the Lagunas for generations, and their economy was slowly shifting away from an agrarian base by the early 1880's. There is evidence that declining agricultural successes were forcing Lagunas to look outside their traditional structure for subsistence.[3] The arrival of the steam locomotive in the Southwest offered alternative employment, which led directly to the departure of many Lagunas from the Pueblo to areas hundreds of miles distant.

Disputes had resulted from the Government's taking of a portion of the Laguna lands near Albuquerque for westward expansion of what would later become the Santa Fe Railroad, during the late nineteenth century. According to Laguna tradition, a compromise was eventually agreed upon, involving the guarantee of Laguna railroad employment on a yearly-renewable basis. This yearly contractual renewal came to be known among the Laguna people as "Watering The Flower." Subsequent renewals confirmed Laguna needs regarding free housing for employees, firewood, travel passes, and other amenities. The paternalism extended in these regards by the Company was not without precedent, as scrap for firewood, free ice, burial plots for workers without family ties, and other considerations, had been a Santa Fe standard beginning in the early 1880's (Ducker 47).

There is a disparity between Laguna remembrance and corroborative data as to whether the original agreement for employment and commodities was ever set out on paper.[4] While no written agreement has been discovered, the Laguna employees believe strongly that an oral contract was made with Santa Fe and continues in force even today. This belief, coupled with the annual renewals—almost

---

[3] "With occasional loss of crops due to floods, the necessity arose, especially after the 1880's, for finding additional means of support from time to time. Work on the railroad which was built through the Pueblo country in the 1880's became available as the Anglo cities increased in population and as various kinds of jobs became available in Albuquerque, Santa Fe...and the many new towns. Outside employment was more and more relied on as a way of making at least a portion of one's living" (Spicer, *Cycles* 176).

ritualisic in aspect—reflects an affirmation of faith that provides the core of mutual accommodation in the Laguna-Santa Fe relationship. The consequent loyalty of the Laguna workers to their employer, based on their 1880 verbal agreement, is clear in the comments of a seventy-year-old retired employee:

A. "Yeah, Santa Fe Railroad agreement on this job.
"Anyway, you come up something like a war, you always call us and need help, we'll help you, you know.
"They take good care of us, and that's a good company, the railroad." (Personal interviews)

Eighty people are gathered in the Laguna Indian Reservation Recreation Hall in New Mexico for a sit-down dinner on the evening of November 14, 1992. This year is the eve of the one-hundred twenty-fifth anniversary of the founding of the Santa Fe Railroad Company (Daggett 127). All of those present have been somehow connected during their lifetimes at the periphery of the Santa Fe. Retirees, wives, children, grandchildren, great-grandchildren, and widows and orphans of deceased Santa Fe workers are sitting down together. It is the first time in the one-hundred and twelve years since the Atchison, Topeka & Santa Fe contracted to employ Lagunas as laborers that a gathering of this kind has taken place. Many express their pleasure, commenting repeatedly: "We thought the Company had forgotten about us." Although there are no Santa Fe representatives present, the dinner guests are nonetheless surprised and happy their former employer has sponsored this reunion dinner.

The reunion was eagerly awaited by most of the participants. A few had tried previously to organize such an event. Working for the Santa Fe brought many alliances, experiences, and memories that are now only partially recalled by fading photographs and news clippings: the Santa Fe All Indian Band, powwows in Golden Gate Park, children playing at night under the dim security lights of the Winslow train yards, a First Communion dinner in a boxcar meeting hall at the Richmond Terminal. The reunion is a chance, hoped by most to be the first of many, for grasping at threads of experiences that are now woven into that seamless cloth of awareness: the persistent sense of being Laguna.

---

[4] For an example, see letters requesting copies of a documented contract, written by the Sacramento Agency, Bureau of Indian Affairs, on behalf of Acoma residents at the Richmond Village; National Archives, Pacific-Sierra Region, Record Group: 75/BIA, Subgroup: Sacramento Area Office, Series: Coded Central Files 1910-1958, Box: 7, Folder: 039 Acoma Pueblo; San Bruno, California.

As the evening progresses, the main course is finished and the participants await dessert. A Native woman rounds up people for photographs, sometimes basing pictures on which of the four tribally recognized Colonies they lived in while away from home. Post World War Two economic changes brought a Company shift in policy toward retaining the housing for the workers. By 1984 the Village at Richmond, as well as the others, had been razed. The diners willingly cluster together for group photos: they are living reminders of their respective Colonies.

The crowd is warming to the food and the occasion, and railroad stories are beginning to occupy the after-dinner time. Reminiscences of living in boxcars converted to homes spill from the smiling faces of two sisters born in the train yards. They nudge each other as one announces proudly "We were born in boxcar number twenty-two." Then laughter all around as her husband shows surprise and says that "She lied to me, told me her family had money and everything. Now I even find out she was born in a boxcar." The wife grins widely, exclaiming "Right. I'm a Boxcar Baby!" Another Laguna, retired back to the Reservation after more than thirty-five years in the Richmond yards, talks about the Village:

> Q. "You all came out there in.?"
> A. "Well, my (husband) went out there,...when did you go out there?(to husband)..in 1942."
> Q. "And about how many people were in the Village at that time?"
> A. "At that time the families weren't out there yet. It was just the menfolks that went out first. There was over a hundred men that were working with Santa Fe."
> Q. "And then the families came on later?"
> A. "Yeah. And there were twenty-nine families besides the bachelors that were out there."
> "Because of the other group that had (already) gone out there, some had gone into the service."
> Q. "Had they volunteered?"
> A. "No, they were drafted." (Personal interviews)

The narrator's husband, a thirty-nine year veteran of the Santa Fe at Richmond, adds:

> "They do pretty good at that time, during the war. The Santa Fe wants Lagunas, so they're out there. About a hundred of them. Some they put on right away, all kinds of mechanics, machinists, on the job that time so, when they start war heavy, then they draft them.
> "Left about thirty more, something like that. I didn't go, you know. Some of the men didn't go 'cause the rest of them all went. And they called some women to go (to Richmond). All Lagunas was working out there. I don't know how many of them, a lot of them working out there." (Personal interviews)

The Richmond narrator of the oral history, Marguerite Williams, had stood at the far edge of an abyss, there in the Laguna boxcar living room. She declared this later, saying that "Santa Fe had those people so cowed that they thought that they were actually doing them a favor letting them live in those little shacks" (Dunning 116). Her perception of the Village's self-identity was obscured when she related that after reporting a firewood gathering expedition to the newspaper, the "Indian women got outraged" by her judgment of their inability to handle their own affairs. The narrator relates their explanation given for the anger:

> M. Williams "They said they understood, but it made it look like they were looking for charity, and that Santa Fe wouldn't go for that. They would be thinking that they were out here begging, and then they would make them go back to the reservation.
> "I had to apologize to them." (Dunning 115)

Family history, personal experience, and intervening years combined to compel the narrator to analyze by her own adopted standards what was observed. The replication of reservation life and values were unseen and unintelligible to the urbanized descendant of a Louisiana slave family. What was observed was perceived as "pitiful" and the boxcar homes were "hovels" when measured through her surveyor's transit of human judgment.

In *American Indian Holocaust And Survival* Russell Thornton states urbanization to be "a process whereby the social norms and cultural values of an urban way of life become transmitted to populations of nonurban areas" (226). Whether or not such norms and values would be absorbed into the sense of being Laguna ultimately depends on the willingness of the receivers to adapt to them. What became lost in the chasm separating divergent world views was that Laguna life in the Richmond Indian Village was full, rich, and not in need of filling up: the cup was already full to running over with the duplicated tribal life of the Laguna Pueblo in New Mexico.

The late Edward Spicer wrote in "Persistent Cultural Systems":

"...a persistent system is a cumulative cultural phenomenon, an open-ended system that defines a course of action for the people believing in it. Such peoples are able to maintain continuity in their experience and their conception of themselves in a wide variety of sociocultural environments." (799)

This type of cultural system, said Spicer, was identifiable by conditions he summarized as an "oppositional process," involving a large-scale organization as the stage setting for the interaction of individuals. He felt such a situation often "produces intense collective consciousness," and a "high degree of internal solidarity," accompanied by motivation for the involved individuals to continue the experience stored symbolically in their identity systems. A persistent sense of being, and remaining, Laguna may therefore be the result of opposition to the urban setting and the intrusion of well-meaning outsiders. Resistance to further non-Laguna inquiry into Village life is heard in the responses from a former boxcar occupant:

Q. "They (the Santa Fe) were good for you?"
A. "Yeah."
Q. "What would you think was the best thing about the Village?"
A. "I don't know."
Q. "Anything you want people to know about the Village?"
A. "No." (Personal interviews)

The core of being Laguna may have adopted Santa Fe employment as one signpost of that being, but such is readable only on Laguna terms, and cannot be understood by anyone not possessing the thousands of other symbolic signifiers of "being Laguna." The Santa Fe Indian Village at Richmond was created from an historic agreement and a migration to respect the intent of that contract. Only this skeletal framework, however, may be viewed, analyzed, and interpreted by others. The mesh and texture of existence in the Santa Fe yards must be measured solely by those for whom the sense of being Laguna represented the practical and spiritual meaning of life, the Boxcar Babies of the Richmond Indian Village.

WORKS CITED

Daggett, Stuart. *Railroad Consolidation West of the Mississippi River.* New York: Arno P, 1981.

Ducker, James H. *Men of the Steel Rails: Workers on the Atchison, Topeka & Santa Fe Railroad 1869-1900.* Lincoln: U of Nebraska P, 1983.

Dunning, Judith K. *Harry and Marguerite Williams: Reflections of a Longtime Black Family in Richmond.* Regional Oral History Office, The Bancroft Library, U of California, Berkeley.

Gregory, James N. *American Exodus: The Dust Bowl Migration and Okie Culture in California.* New York: Oxford UP, 1989.

Labor Conflict in the United States: An Encyclopedia. Ed. Ronald L. Filippelli. New York: Garland Publishing, 1990.

Meriam, Lewis, Technical Director. *The Problem of Indian Administration: Report of a Survey made at the request of Honorable Hubert Work. Secretary 1928 of the Interior, submitted to him. February 21, 1928.* Institute for Government Research. Baltimore: Johns Hopkins UP.

Rands, Robert. "Ethnography of the Southwest" in *American Indian Ethnohistory: Indians of the Southwest.* Ed. David Agee Horr. Vols. 3-5. New York: Garland Publishing, Inc., 1974.

Scott, Mel. *The San Francisco Bay Area: A Metropolis in Perspective.* Berkeley: U of California P, 1985.

Spicer, Edward H. *Cycles of Conquest.* Tucson: U of Arizon 1989.

____. "Persistent Cultural Systems." *Science,* 174, no. 19 (Nov. 1971).

Thornton, Russell. *American Indian Holocaust and Survival: A Population History Since 1492.* Norman: U of Oklahoma P, 1987.

Waters, L. L. *Steel Trails to Santa Fe.* Lawrence: U of Kansas P, 1950.

Gerald Vizenor's Shadow Plays: Narrative Mediations and Multiplicities of Power

Juana Maria Rodriguez, University of California, Berkeley

In 1967, Thomas James White Hawk, a Dakota Indian, was indicted, charged and pled guilty to the murder of James Yeado, a white jeweler, and the rape of his wife. He was sentenced, without trial, to death by electrocution. In the aftermath of these events, Gerald Vizenor, working as a journalist at the time, wrote and distributed thousands of pamphlets publicizing the details of the case and mobilizing support for repeal of the death sentence.[1] Two years later, White Hawk's sentence was commuted to life imprisonment without parole. It was suggested that the controversy surrounding the case had hurt the state's tourism during hunting season.

At first read, "Thomas White Hawk" is a straightforward narrative of murder in post colonial[2] America, another Bigger Thomas caught in the web of someone else's nightmare. Gerald Vizenor, enters in the role of narrative mediator, who, acting through the authority of the text, intervenes to effect communication and renegotiate the terms of the discourse. There is a life at stake. The immediate goal is having White Hawk's death sentence changed to one of life imprisonment. Through the publication and dissemination of the story, this goal is attained: White Hawk's sentence is commuted to life imprisonment without parole. Both the life of Thomas White Hawk and the right of white men to hunt other game in South Dakota, free of Indian protests and controversy, are preserved. But the story

---

[1] This pamphlet, edited as an article and entitled "Thomas White Hawk" was reprinted with the addendum "Commutation of Death," in Gerald Vizenor's collection, *Cross Bloods: Bone Courts, Bingo and Other Reports.*

[2] I use post colonial here in the sense of after the on-set of colonialism. See *The Empire Writes Back: Theory and Practice in Post-Colonial Literatures.*

and the storyteller remain to unravel the fabric of relations that constitute power.

This paper will analyze the ways in which multiple relations of power compete within preexisting narratives. In the process, I will attempt to disentangle the ways in which these discursive spaces are defined and the various ways in which power is exercised within them. Foucault challenges the paradigm that defines power as a "general system of domination exerted by one group over another." Instead, he writes,

> Power is not an institution, and not a structure; neither is it a certain strength we are endowed with; it is the name one attributes to a complex strategical situation in a particular society. (*History of Sexuality* 92-93)

The texts that comprise the case of Thomas White Hawk will be explored in several ways. I will begin by examining the ways in which the multiple subject of White Hawk acts, reacts and is acted upon within an interwoven system of power relations. Power within this context consists of both individual and institutional power. In this case, institutional power extends to encompass the reservation, the courts, fosterage and guardian systems, educational systems, prisons, churches, families, and psychiatric institutions. Secondly, I will analyze the ways in which the story of this multiple subject is written, negotiated, and inscribed by a multitude of discursive systems including psychiatry, law, feminism, and an American Indian national liberation movement. Finally, I will examine the ways in which different narrative styles employed by Vizenor illuminate and shadow elements of the story.

In "Thomas White Hawk," Vizenor begins the story with the last details of James Yeado's life. It is an intimate portrait: the narrator tells us that Yeado was a Virgo, a gardener, the father of two children, and a member of the Vermillion Chamber of Commerce. On the opposite page is a copy of a handwritten note with the words "Notes Pertaining to My Case" scribbled across the top. Its author is not identified, but we know it is Yeado's murderer.

Vizenor first introduces us to Thomas James White Hawk a few paragraphs later, identified as a freshman premed student. He writes:

> Yeado had sold a good many engagement rings to University students, but this one was different. He knew them both. They were Indians. (102)

The last two lines are short and deliberate, and the sequence seems noteworthy. The narrator does not refer to these Indians by tribe or speculate as to the source of Yeado's knowledge. The sentences seem somewhat connected, yet the construction is never stated. By beginning from the perspective of Yeado, the narrator creates a sense of textual distance and neutrality from White Hawk, and compassion for the murder victim.

Vizenor's construction of White Hawk seems slow and deliberate. Bits and pieces of his life are interspersed between vivid details of the crime and the ensuing events of the trial. White Hawk the murderer, the rapist, the Indian, becomes layered with other vestments of identity. A Dakota born on the Rosebud reservation, an orphan who had lived under the care of white people for most of his life, a football player and track star who had suffered an injury to the head many years back, a young man who dreams of being a doctor.

The omniscient narrator never hints at the source of his construction. Some of the details are mundane, others more profound. Many incidents are only suggested in the text, yet the suggestions are revealing, beginning with the possible murder of his mother, "Friends have told him that his mother died in childbirth, but he has dreams that she died some other way" (111). Later, White Hawk's guardian is introduced with the portentous line "*Phil Zoubek...is Tom's guardian and a lot more.* Each of these two men is half of a warm human adventure" (115). Zoubek's name and the words "a lot more" are italicized in the text, as if to make explicit the homosexual relationship they shared. The source of this knowledge is again kept hidden, creating a textual silence and raising further questions as to the *actual* nature of this relationship between a white foster father and his teenage Indian son.

Other instances of italicized text point the reader to discursive contradictions, phrases such as "*cultural norms,*" "*uncontrolled discretion,*" or Judge Bandy's euphemism for capital punishment, "*I am removing you from the world.*" This selective glossing visually marks the text with authorial intention and disrupts the illusion of journalistic objectivity and distance. Vizenor exercises his authorial power through the coded text and its dissemination. It is ultimately this power which 'saves' White Hawk from the death sentence.

Already the relationships of power have begun to breed: White Hawk's power over James Yeado and his wife, Zoubek's power over White Hawk, the power of the fosterage system, the courts, the educational system, and of course the authorial power of the text. A Foucaultian nightmare of competing discourses acted out on the body of Thomas White Hawk.

In much of his writings, Foucault demonstrates the interdependence of the penal and medical systems in terms of creating mutually supportive discourses on criminality, deviance, and delinquency. In *Discipline and Punish: The Birth of the Prison*, Foucault delineates the history of the penal system in the West. He argues that it is the person, not the crime that is judged and punished. He writes:

> Certainly the 'crimes' and 'offenses' on which judgement is passed are judicial objects defined by the code, but judgement is also passed on the passions, instincts, anomalies, infirmities, maladjustments, effects of environment or heredity; acts of aggression are punished, so also, through them is aggressivity, rape, but at the same time perversions; murders, but also drives and desires... For it is these shadows lurking behind the case itself that are judged and punished... [A]nd which, behind the pretext of explaining an action, are ways of defining an individual. (17-18)

White Hawk's trial inevitably becomes dependent on the sanity of the defendant. The judicial-psychiatric discourse surrounding the trial was perhaps the most verbose in its depiction of him. Terms such as "psychoneurotic", "sociopathic," "*passive-aggressive*," and "personality defect" with a "*poor prognosis in treatment*" were all used to describe and define White Hawk. The legally imposed binary of guilty or innocent becomes dependent on the psychiatric binary of sane or insane. Psychiatry helps to create the narrative of victim turned victimizer, "the result of '*environmental contacts*.'" A "personality disturbance [which] appears to be his ambivalence concerning his psychosexual development." This White Hawk, constructed through a psychiatric discourse, seems to take on the characteristics of an odd sort of Oedipus, murdering the figure of the white paternal father and sleeping with the forbidden mother.

Other preexisting narratives have already circumscribed White Hawk's story.[3] Each represses aspects of the subject's positionality, and tries to reinscribe the story within a specific narrative which is always already written in binary opposites. These arguments are in turn instrumental in reconstructing the binary of victimization and agency, innocence or guilt. They include:

1. The colonial narrative which inscribes the story in terms of civilization/savagery, christian/heathen. Within this narrative, White Hawk's crime is etched into the dominant psyche as an act of treason against the purity of a white social order and must be punishable by death. How would the trial and the sentence have been different if the Yeados were Chinese, African

---

[3] For an example of how preexisting narratives frame political arguments see Lata Mani.

American, Indian?

2. The cultural nationalist narrative which reads White Hawk as a victim of the hegemonic powers that seek to destroy him. This anti-colonial narrative challenges the occupying state's authority to define criminality, sanity, and jurisdiction. His act is thus inscribed as an act of rebellion against the dominant culture. However, in this narrative the male nationalist fantasy of ultimate revenge thus becomes coded as murdering the white man and sleeping with his wife. Indian vs. White Man.

3. An unwritten radical white feminist narrative which would write White Hawk as a victimizer of women. The act of rape is written as purely an act of male violence, the ultimate expression of patriarchal power. White Hawk is thus written as an agent of male power. The white woman is then revealed as a pawn between the Native man and the white man. Man vs. Woman. However, these terms are already racialized: Native Man, white woman, obfuscating the figure of the white man. In both this and previous scenarios, the Native woman is totally written out of the story.

Vizenor draws on these competing discourses to construct the complexity of social forces impacting the fate of the multiple subject. The origins of these narratives are as old and as new as the binary of 'us' and 'them.' They circulate like viruses, infiltrating the body politic. In contrast, Vizenor deconstructs the tyranny of these preexisting binaries by presenting a multiplicity of voices and power relations. Nowhere in the text is it suggested that White Hawk views *himself* as a colonialized subject, or as an agent against cultural hegemony, or white womanhood. These narratives have been constructed by others for their own ends, and White Hawk is merely caught in their web.

White Hawk's participation in the crime is never contested; instead, the text attempts to challenge absolute definitions of agency and victimization. In order to do so, the multiple subject must then be repositioned within a legion of oppressive localities. White Hawk as colonized male subject, childhood victim, murderer, rapist, is already racialized and gendered within existing systems of power. These factors exist simultaneously, even as they contradict and contest each other's power to define. This is where Foucault's theories of power as omnipresent and capillary are most productive. Rather than seeing power as something that is held by a centralized force (state or patriarchy), it is something which is fluid and dynamic, something that is exercised rather than possessed.

The omnipresence of power: not because it has the privilege of consolidating everything under its invincible unity, but because it is produced from one moment
to the next, at every point. Power is everywhere; not because it embraces everything, but because it comes from everywhere. (*History of Sexuality* 93)

Foucault's work does not deny or minimize the power of the state and its institutions; however, he sees this as only one form of power. By recognizing the fluidity
of power he is also able to acknowledge the swarm of power relations that operate
on the microlevel of society.

By presenting the case in its fullest complexity, Vizenor is able to capture these
subtleties of power and use them to mediate between the several narratives that I
have delineated. Vizenor puts flesh on the multiple subject and attempts to repo-
sition White Hawk as a Dakota Indian within post-colonial occupied America. He
gives us pictures of White Hawk, of downtown Vermillion, photographs of each of
the central characters in the trial in an attempt to make them something more than
the individual roles they play. There are no photos of Yeado and his wife. They are
incidental characters, whose actions appear offstage and are only alluded to in the
text; they have no agency and no voice in this new story of crime and punishment.

Instead, Vizenor's narrative remains focused on White Hawk. His discursive
power lies in his ability to reframe judicial and psychiatric discourses in terms of
colonialism and power. This would include the diagnosis of White Hawk as suffer-
ing from cultural schizophrenia and the coding of Zoubek as homosexual.
Throughout the court transcripts, Vizenor again inserts italicized text that is at
times White Hawk's memories, dreams and thoughts and at other times, the
thoughts of Judge Bandy and others. These glossed phrases suggest a discursive ex-
cess which can not be expressed within the prefigured legal or psychiatric framework.

Vizenor's investment and fascination with White Hawk, beyond the goal of
commutation, hints at motives within the shadows of the lines. The question mark
that is intent curves ambiguously around each sentence and textual silence. Each
time the story is told it becomes transformed. The story becomes multiple, radiat-
ing out to encompass the other stories circulating around White Hawk. With each
new telling, the position of the narrator shifts.

Vizenor is first and foremost a storyteller. In his writings, the man slips in and
out of the shadows he projects. In a recent piece, "The Ruins of Representation"
Vizenor uses the term "shadow survivance" as a means to understand tribal consciousness and literatures. He writes,

The shadow is that sense of intransitive motion to the referent; the silence in memories. Shadows are neither the absence of entities nor the burden of conceptual references. The shadow is the silence that inherits the words, shadows are the motions that mean the silence, but not the presence or absence of entities. (1)

It is these shadows that inhabit his own texts.

The story is first told in "Thomas White Hawk" as a seemingly nonfictional piece of journalism, printed as a pamphlet and later reprinted as a collection *Crossbloods: Bone Courts, Bingo and Other Reports*. In the piece, Vizenor assumes the role of omniscient narrator. He withholds the political intent of his text which is clearly the commutation of White Hawk's death sentence. Intent is also related to Vizenor's masking his own subject position. Like White Hawk, Vizenor is a tribal mixed blood survivor of cultural schizophrenia, the foster care system and childhood abuse and neglect. Vizenor's naming himself as a survivor would have further implicated White Hawk's own agency: Good Indian vs. Bad Indian. By cloaking his role as writer and investigator, as well as his connection and insight to White Hawk's past, he veils the sources of his knowledge. After the immediate goal of commutation has been achieved, other stories can be told.

In the collection *Crossbloods*, this first telling is directly followed by the short piece entitled "Commutation of Death," a polemic on the limits of justice in occupied territories. In this piece, Vizenor writes:

[T]he story will not end because White Hawk has become a symbol of the conflicts and injustices of many *dakota* people living in a white-dominated state. And the dominant white people on the plains will not forget the savage demon who twice raped a white woman while her husband was dying of gunshot wounds in the next room. (152)

In this addendum, the narrator is unrestrained by the limits of advocacy journalism, and the subsequent problems of audience and authorial motivation. He is able to point directly to the intent of the text, without the concern of alienating many of the white liberals it was intended to sway. Once the immediacy of commuting White Hawk's sentence has been achieved, the narrator is free to move outside the specificities of the case and address the larger issues of justice and white domination.

In *Wordarrows: Indians and Whites in the New Fur Trade*, the story is retold in a series of veiled fictionalized accounts which allow for details, previously considered marginal, unspeakable or unsubstantiated to be told under the guise of fiction. As the story moves farther away from the scene of White Hawk's crime, the image of the author and his own investment and attraction to the stories become clearer.

In the series of stories in *Wordarrows*, Vizenor inserts himself in the text under the name of Clement Beaulieu, a "liberal tribal writer." Clement Beaulieu is the name of Vizenor's grandfather, and Clement is also the name of his father, who was himself the victim of a seemingly senseless murder. The intertextuality that exists between these stories adds credence and depth to the original story of the trial as they explicate the complexities of Indian identity.

By creating himself through the character Beaulieu, Vizenor gives voice to the ethnic identity that he shares with White Hawk. Vizenor transforms himself through this character to escape representations of the author. Fiction allows for the articulation of this Native voice which would have further complicated the initial narrative of White Hawk's trial. Yet, even here, Beaulieu is one character, one voice, among many. The position of both the narrator and the author remains shadowed.

The stories in *Word Arrows* have as much to do with the writer's search for a way to understand White Hawk's story as with the case itself. Here, Vizenor delves even deeper into the microlevel of power relations circulating around the trial. Among the stories woven around the figure of White Hawk is the illicit affair between the minister's wife and the condemned man through the bars of a prison cell, a Pine Ridge Indian law student who testifies for the prosecution as an expert on tribal justice in support of capital punishment, and Beaulieu's invisibility as a tribal person which allows others to speak uncensored about the Indians in their midst. The characters he invokes, are marginal at best to the narratives I have delineated, yet they reveal the many ways in which Native peoples are made savage, exotic, invisible, insane within the dominant culture.

In a third, and as yet unfinished future telling of the story, Vizenor plans to reinsert himself through the use of first person narration. Yet, even from within this posture, the 'real' author remains in the shadows. Even within the genre of personal testimony through autobiography, the author remains the fictive construction of authorial imagination, as evidenced by the subtitle of Vizenor's own autobiography, *Interior Landscapes: Autobiographical Myths and Metaphors*. In a recent work, Vizenor writes "[F]irst person pronouns have no referent. The other is a continuous pronoun with no shadow" ("The Ruins of Representation" 20).

Through narrative, Vizenor is able to deconstruct binary representations of subjectivity. By presenting a range of competing discourses, he challenges the authority of others to define, and hence judge. By occupying the shadows, he makes sense of the multitude of discursive statements and silences surrounding the case. Narrative ultimately allows him a way to mediate between the vestiges of language that exist between the binaries.

WORKS CITED

Ashcroft, Bill, Gareth Griffiths, and Helen Tifflin, eds. *The Empire Writes Back: Theory and Practice in Post-Colonial Literatures.* London: Routledge, 1989.

Foucault, Michel. *Discipline and Punish: Birth of the Prison.* Trans. Alan Sheridan. New York: Vintage Books, 1979.

___. *The History of Sexuality: Volume I, An Introduction.* Trans. Robert Hurley. New York: Vintage Books, 1990.

Mani, Lata. "Multiple Mediations: Feminist Scholarship in the Age of Multinational Reception." *Feminist Review* 35 Summer 1990: 24-39.

Vizenor, Gerald. "The Ruins of Representation: Shadow Survivance and the Literature of Dominance." Unpublished typescript, October 1992.

___. *Cross Bloods: Bone Courts, Bingo and Other Reports.* Minneapolis: U of Minnesota P, 1990.

___. *Interior Landscapes: Autobiographical Myths and Metaphors.* Minneapolis: U of Minnesota P, 1990.

___. *Wordarrows: Indians and Whites in the New Fur Trade.* Minneapolis: U of Minnesota P, 1978.

Native American Indian Identities: Autoinscriptions and the Cultures of Names

Gerald Vizenor, *University of California, Berkeley*

Native American Indian identities bear the memories and solace of heard stories; the cultures of tribal identities are inscrutable creations, an innermost brush with natural reason, and, at the same time, unbounded narcissism and the tease of pretensions.

William Least Heat-Moon, for instance, the author of *Blue Highways*, assumed a surname and then embraced pronouns that would undermine his own postindian identities.

Heat-Moon, in the foreword to the new edition of *Old Indian Trails* by Walter McClintock, simulated the presence of the tribal other, with a rhetorical wish to "live as the Indians did before the Europeans descended here. Perhaps even better, to join a tribe with old ways and discover whether life with people only slightly beyond a stone-age culture is sweeter than ours, to learn whether tribal Americans truly built their lives around a harmony and balance between humankind and the rest of nature."

The sources of some postindian identities have become texts, an unheard consumer renaissance of scriptural performances. Kenneth Lincoln, and others, celebrate modernist communal adoptions; Hertha Wong, on the other hand, seems to search for an essential tribal connection; and Jamake Highwater simulates his elusive tribal descent as an author.

Traditional Native American Indian names are heard in visions and conceived in performances: sacred names are private, and most nicknames are based on performances and communal experiences as the sources of identities. Traditional nicknames, however, are seldom autoinscriptions; most descriptive nicknames are given by peers not publishers.

The autoinscriptions of postindian nicknames are texts, commercial instruments that endorse the simulations of identities in the absence of the heard, and the absence of performance, or memories of the tribal real. The observance of heard stories once situated tribal names and remembrance. Now, as identities become textual commodities, certain authors inscribe their own descriptive names and then, as a postindian reversal of a traditional encore, enact the text or autoinscription as a simulation of identities. Doubtless some "traditions" are invented to support the texts of postindian identities. Traditions and names, in this sense, serve the literature of dominance not tribal survivance.

The sources of tribal remembrance, creation, personal visions, tragic wisdom, and the communal nature of the heard are precarious, but the capacities and nuances of posted names are burdened more with colonial discoveries, the duplicities of dominance, and pretentious simulations, than with the menace of silence, the inaccuracies of memories, or the uncertainties of stories out of season.

The distinctive salutations of a personal tribal nature, however, are more than the mere translation and possession of memories and names. Consider the untold influences and choices in specific cultural experiences, and the various sources of identities in public, private, intimate, and sacred circumstances; the choices become even more enigmatic with the vagaries, pleasures, and treasons of cultural contact, and the transvaluations of such wicked notions as savagism and civilization in the course of histories.

The literatures of dominance, the histories, narratives of discoveries, translations, cultural studies, and prescribed names of time, place, and person, are treacherous conditions in any discourse on tribal consciousness. The poses of silence are not natural, and other extremes, such as cultural revisionism, the ironic eminence of sacred consumer names, and assumed tribal nicknames, are sources of identities besides the obvious associations; these distinctions, poses, adoptions, imitations, and other maneuvers, are unsure scriptural stories told over and over in common conversations of dominance.

Natural reason and survivance are active representations of the rights of consciousness; the romantic adoption of tribal names and identities is passive and serves the causes of dominance.

Sacred names, those secure ceremonial names, were scarcely heard by missionaries or government agents and seldom translated as surnames; nicknames were assured in tribal stories, but the stories were lost in translation as surnames.

Later, most surnames were chosen and dictated at federal and mission schools. Some tribal names endure in stories, and nicknames are identities learned and ascertained in the performance of stories; moreover, descriptive names seem to be more esteemed in translation, and certain choices of names are mere simulations with no active memories or stories.

Snowarrow is but one recent name that has been chosen by a teacher to augment his tribal identities. Youngblood is another; some nicknames are ostentatious, and others are read with no ascriptions. Some names are eschewed and renounced for countless reasons. Thomas Edward Kill, for instance, petitioned a court for legal permission to change his surname because he hoped to become a medical doctor and he did not think his tribal name in translation would inspire confidence.

Kenneth Lincoln avows adoption as a source of significance as a scholar. He noted in *Indi'n Humor* that "he was adopted into the Oglala Sioux." The sapient humor of adoption is elusive, a passive simulation, and a dubious endorsement of authenticity.

Some names and associations are chance, to be sure, an ironic observance, or the break even consciousness of apostates; for all that, tribal stories and natural reason are unanimous, memorable even in translation, and descriptive names are so celebrated in this generation that thousands of "wannabee" romantics pursue an obscure tribal connection, an adoption, a passive wisp of ancestral descent in a document or name. Others bear consumer simulations and pretensions as personal identities, for various reasons, and pretend to be tribal in the name, blood, and remembrance of those who have endured racialism and the literatures of dominance.

Native American Indian identities are created in stories, and names are essential to a distinctive personal nature, but memories, visions, and the shadows of heard stories are the paramount verities of a tribal presence. The shadows are active and intransitive, the visual memories that are heard as tribal stories; these memories are trusted to sacred names and tribal nicknames.

Tribal identities would have no existence without active choices, the choices that are heard in stories and mediated in names; otherwise, tribal identities might be read as mere simulations of remembrance. The literatures of dominance are dubious entitlements to the names in other cultures, simulations that antecede the shadows of the real and then unteach the mediations of tribal names and stories.

Luther Standing Bear, for instance, chose his names, and the stories of the bear are heard even in the translation of his surname. He wrote in *My Indian Boyhood* that the "Indian very seldom bothers a bear and the bear, being a very self-respecting and peaceful animal, seldom bothers a human being." The bear is the shadow in the memories and the trace in his names. The bear is "so much like a human that he is interesting to watch. He has a large amount of human vanity and likes to look at himself." The bear is "wise and clever and he probably knows it."

Not only is the bear "a powerful animal in body, but powerful in will also." The bear "will stand and fight to the last. Though wounded, he will not run, but will die fighting. Because my father shared this spirit with the bear, he earned his name," wrote Standing Bear.

N. Scott Momaday, the novelist, wrote in *The Way to Rainy Mountain* that his tribal grandmother "lived out her long life in the shadow of Rainy Mountain, the immense landscape of the continental interior lay like memory in her blood. She could tell of the Crows, whom she had never seen, and of the Black Hills, where she had never been. I wanted to see in reality what she had seen more perfectly in the mind's eye, and traveled fifteen hundred miles to begin my pilgrimage." Aho, his grandmother, heard stories of a migration that lasted five centuries; she could hear and see a landscape, and these stories became the shadows of tribal imagination and remembrance.

Momaday honors the memories of his grandmother and touches the shadows of his own imagination; shadows that trace his identities and tribal stories in three scriptural themes in *The Way to Rainy Mountain*.

Tribal nicknames are the shadows heard in stories; the pleasures of nicknames, even in translation, are an unmistakable celebration of personal identities. Nicknames are personal stories that would, to be sure, trace the individual to tribal communities rather than cause separations by pronouns of singular recognition.

Brian Swann and Arnold Krupat, the editors of *I Tell You Now: Autobiographical Essays by Native American Writers,* pointed out that the "notion of telling the whole of any one individual's life or taking merely personal experience as of particular significance was, in the most literal way, foreign to them, if not also repugnant." Nothing, however, is foreign or repugnant in personal names and the stories of nicknames. The risks, natural reasons, and praise of visions are sources of personal power in tribal consciousness; personal stories are coherent and name individual identities within communities, and are not an obvious opposition to communal values.

The shadows of personal visions, for instance, were heard and seen alone, but not in cultural isolation or separation from tribal communities. Those who chose to hear visions, an extreme mediation, were aware that their creative encounters with nature were precarious and would be sanctioned by the tribe; personal visions could be of service to tribal families. Some personal visions and stories have the power to heal and liberate the spirit, and there are similar encounters with tribal shadows in the stories written by contemporary Native American Indian authors.

Nicknames, shadows, and shamanic visions, are tribal stories that are heard and remembered as survivance. These personal identities and stories are not the same as those translated in the literatures of dominance.

"My spirit was quiet there," Momaday wrote in *The Names*, a meticulous memoir of his childhood at Jemez, New Mexico. "The silence was old, immediate, and pervasive, and there was great good in it. The wind of the canyons drew it out; the voices of the village carried and were lost in it. Much was made of the silence; much of the summer and winter was made of it."

"I tell parts of my stories here because I have often searched out other lives similar to my own," wrote Linda Hogan in *I Tell You Now*, edited by Brian Swann and Arnold Krupat. "Telling our lives is important, for those who come after us, for those who will see our experience as part of their own historical struggle."

"I was raised by an English-German mother. My father, one-quarter Cherokee, was there also, but it was my mother who presented her white part of my heritage as whole," wrote Diane Glancy in *I Tell You Now*. "I knew I was different, then as much as now. But I didn't know until later that it was because I am part heir to the Indian culture, and even that small part has leavened the whole lump."

"Facts: May 7, 1948. Oakland. Catholic Hospital. Midwife nun, no doctor. Citation won the Kentucky Derby. Israel was born. The United Nations met for the first time," wrote Wendy Rose in *I Tell You Now*. "I have heard Indians joke about those who act as if they had no relatives. I wince, because I have no relatives. They live, but they threw me away. . . . I am without relations. I have always swung back and forth between alienation and relatedness."

"So I was born in Southern Calfornia but I don't remember it. At least not consciously. My mother used to tell me how the roar of the ocean disturbed her at night when we lived in Oceanside, made her feel uneasy somehow. But I have always loved the sound of the ocean," wrote Janet Campbell Hale in *Bloodlines: Odyssey of a Native Daughter*. "In June, when I was six months old, when northern Idaho's harsh winter had ended, my family packed up the car again and left sunny Southern California and went home to where their hearts were.

"I first saw the light of day in California, but the first place I remember is our home in Idaho. There is no place on earth more beautiful than Coeur d'Alene county."

"George Raft was an inspiration to my mother and, in a sense, he was responsible for my conception," wrote Gerald Vizenor in *Interior Landscapes: Autobiographical Myths and Metaphors*. "She saw the thirties screen star, a dark social hero with moral courage, in the spirited manner of my father, a newcomer from the White Earth Reservation. . . . I was conceived on a cold night in a kerosene heated tenement near downtown Minneapolis. President Franklin Delano Roosevelt had been inaugurated the year before, at the depth of the Great Depression. He told the nation, 'The only thing we have to fear is fear itself.' My mother, and millions of other women stranded in cold rooms, heard the new president, listened to their new men, and were roused to remember the movies; elected politicians turned economies, but the bright lights in the depression came from the romantic and glamorous screen stars."

Native American Indian creation stories are in continuous translations, interpretations, and representations; at the same time, postindian simulations and pretensions are abetted as lateral sources of identities. The absence of the heard in translation antecedes a presence in the shadows and hermeneutics of tribal names and stories.

Has the absence of the heard in tribal stories turned to the literatures of dominance? What are the real names, nouns, and pronouns, heard in the unnamable cultures of tribal consciousness? How can a pronoun be a source of tribal identities in translation? How can a pronoun be essential, an inscription of absence that represents the presence of sound and a person in translation?

Simulations are silence, the absence of tragic wisdom; tribal pretensions and political adoptions are passive postscripts without tragic wisdom or the rights of consciousness.

Kenneth Lincoln mentions his adoption on the cover of *Indi'n Humor*. The allusion to a tribal presence suggests that the interpretations of the author are more authentic. Why else would a university professor pose as the other by adoption?

The insinuation of authenticity by adoption is obscure, passive, and indecorous; the pose is a renaissance language game. The mere written words, of course, are postindian simulations not tribal representations. The diverse cultures of tribal identities are not heard as passive pretensions of adoption.

Brian Stock pointed out in *Listening for the Text* that in the occidental world, as "the written word came to play a more important role in law, administration, and commerce, existing oral traditions either declined or adapted to a new environment." In the tribal world, however, the burdens of colonialism, translation, and racialism, denied the natural reason of shared values in the new environment of scriptural dominance.

Luther Standing Bear enacted survivance over dominance at the turn of the last century; he and many other tribal people performed with distinction at federal schools and enacted written words to bear the shadows of their own traditional heard stories.

"Performative acts in language remained verbal, and individualistic, as they had always been," argued Stock. "But they were increasingly contextualized by writing in a manner that implied shared values, assumptions and modes of explanation." Later, these natural connections between literature and society were weakened by structuralism and other theories. "The leading proponents seemed to say: if social relationships cannot be revealed through texts, then we will study the properties of texts for their own sake and pretend that we are studying society." The context of this observation, and the denial of tribal imagination, would embolden textual simulations, the pretensions of adoption, and the autoinscriptions of tribal names in the absence of heard stories.

Indi'n Humor: Bicultural Play in Native America is a contradiction in humor: the poses and intimations of the adoptee become the very ironies of trickster literature. The author is his own reduction, an unwitting reversal of the aesthetic trickster. The simulations of the adoptee are both the subject and the object of his own interpretations; the poses of a schlemiehl or trickster of the modern canon. The author could have been more self-reflexive of his adoption and the distinctions of communal humor, and he could have been more aware of postcolonial tragic wisdom. "My own argument for tribal comic wisdom takes heart from the heyoka, or sacred clown, vision on the western high plains, among the Lakota where I grew up in Nebraska," he wrote. "*Indi'n Humor* takes its cues from literary craftspeople. It is less about criticism than culture, more in search of imaginative spark than speculative certainty."

George Steiner observed in the introduction to a recent edition of *The Trial* by Franz Kafka that "nearly all mature aesthetic form" is self-reflexive. Kafka, in this sense, has more in common with the imagination of Native American Indian authors than the intimations and interpretations of Kenneth Lincoln. "There is a sense in which works of the imagination of sufficient seriousness and density always enact a reflection on themselves," wrote Steiner. "Almost always, the major text or work of art or musical composition tells critically of its own genesis." The imagination of trickster stories enacts a similar reflection and awareness of creation.

Franz Kafka was heir to an "unending analysis," noted Steiner. "The techniques of teasing out the abyss, of circling the unnamable, of weaving meaning on meaning, of labouring to make language wholly transparent to a light which consumes that through which it passes, having their antecedent and validation in the twice-millennary debates of Judaism with itself." Native American Indian literature teases the same imagination of the unnamable, and the light passes through translation, interpretation, reductions, and the insinuations of authenticity.

"Schlemiehls are fools who believe themselves to be in control of their fictive world but are shown to the reader or audience to be in control of nothing, not even themselves," wrote Sander Gilman in *Inscribing the Other*. "Schlemiehls are fools who are branded with the external sign of a deranged language, a language that entraps them." The avowal of adoption brands the author with simulations, the "external signs" of his own interpretations. The trickster created the schlemiehl and the practice of political adoptions to distract those who lack the imagination and tragic wisdom of their own culture of identities.

Hertha Dawn Wong declared an obscure connection to tribal identities in the preface to *Sending My Heart Back Across the Years*, a study of "nonwritten forms of personal narratives." She wrote that "according to the Oklahoma Historical Society, my great-grandfather may have been Creek or Chickasaw or Choctaw or perhaps Cherokee." That whimsical sense of chance, "may have been" one of four or more distinct tribes, is not an answerable choice or active source of credible identities. "I had little idea," when she began writing her book, "that I was part Native American, one of the unidentified mixed-bloods whose forebears wandered away from their fractured communities, leaving little cultural trace in their adopted world." The racialism of these romantic notions are the simulations of dominance.

Elizabeth Cook-Lynn, editor of *Wicazo Sa Review*, argued that the "wannabee sentiment" that clutters *Sending My Heart Back Across the Years* "is a reflection of a growing phenomenon" at universities in "the name of Native American Studies." The "unnecessary claim of this scholar to be 'part Native American' is so absurd as to cast ridicule on the work itself." She pointed out that curriculum development at universities "has been reduced to offerings which might be called 'What If I'm a Little Bit Indian?'" The pretensions of some scholars, however, are not even a little bit Indian.

Jack Anderson, in a column released by the Universal Press Syndicate in 1984, reported that Jamake Highwater, "one of the country's most celebrated Indians has fabricated much of the background that made him famous." Highwater, the columnist revealed, "lied about many details of his life. Asked why someone of such genuine and extraordinary talent felt he had to concoct a spurious background, Highwater said he felt that doors would not have opened for him if he had relied on his talent alone." Anderson pointed out that "Vine Deloria Jr. and Hank Adams say flatly that Highwater is not an Indian."

Highwater, author of *The Primal Mind* and other books about tribal cultures, may have opened doors with his spurious identities, but he also stole public attention, and his bent for recognition may have closed some doors on honest tribal people who have the moral courage to raise doubts about the cultures and simulations of identities. "The greatest mystery of my life is my own identity," Highwater wrote in *Shadow Show: An Autobiographical Insinuation*, published two years after the column by Jack Anderson. "To escape things that are painful we must reinvent ourselves. Either we reinvent ourselves or we choose not to be anyone at all. We must not feel guilty if we are among those who have managed to survive."

Highwater was very active in his tribal simulations, but the poses were in the cause of dominance. Imagination and active reflection would be honorable considerations if the author had not been deceptive about his past. At last he can write about his performance as the other, and the ease of his lonesome poses in the theater of dominance.

Anthony Kerby argued in *Narrative and the Self* that the loss of the "ability to narrate one's past is tantamount to a form of amnesia, with a resultant diminishing of one's sense of self. Why should this be so? The answer, broadly stated, is that our history constitutes a drama in which we are a leading character, and the meaning of this role is to be found only through the recollective and imaginative configuring of that history in autobiographical acts. In other words, in narrating the past we understand ourselves to be the implied subject generated by the narrative."

In other words, the cultures of tribal identities are heard in names and stories; otherwise the simulations that antecede tribal stories and tragic wisdom would be tantamount to the amnesia of discoveries in the literatures of dominance.

WORKS CITED

Gilman, Sander. *Inscribing the Other.* Lincoln: U of Nebraksa P, 1991.

Hale, Janet Campbell. *Bloodlines: Odyssey of a Native Daughter.* New York: Random House, 1993.

Least Heat-Moon, William, foreword. *Old Indian Trails.* By Walter McLintock. New York: Houghton Mifflin Co, 1992.

Highwater, Jamake. *Shadow Show: An Autobiographical Insinuation.* New York: Alfred van der Marck Editions, 1986.

Kerby, Anthony. *Narrative and the Self.* Bloomington: Indiana UP, 1991 .

Lincoln, Kenneth. *Indi'n Humor: Bicultural Play in Native America.* New York: Oxford UP, 1993.

Momaday, N. Scott. *The Way to Rainy Mountain.* Albuquerque: U of New Mexico P, 1969.

___. *The Names.* New York: Harper & Row, 1976.

Standing Bear, Luther. *My Indian Boyhood.* Lincoln: U of Nebraska P, 1931.

Steiner, George, introd. *The Trial.* By Franz Kafka. New York: Everyman's Library, Alfred A. Knopf, 1992.

Stock, Brian. *Listening for the Text.* Baltimore: The Johns Hopkins UP, 1990.

Swann, Brian and Arnold Krupat, eds. *I Tell You Now: Autobiographical Essays by Native American Writers.* Lincoln: U of Nebraska P, 1987.

Vizenor, Gerald. *Interior Landscapes: Autobiographical Myths and Metaphors.* Minneapolis: U of Minnesota P, 1990.

Wong, Hertha Dawn. *Sending My Heart Across the Years.* New York: Oxford UP, 1992.

Contributors

Robert Berner
Professor Emeritus of English,
University of Wisconsin, Oshkosh

Kimberly M. Blaeser (Chippewa)
Department of English,
University of Wisconsin, Milwaukee

Helen Jaskoski
Department of English,
California State University, Fullerton

Kurt M. Peters (Blackfeet and Powhatan)
Postdoctoral student in American Indian Studies Center,
University of California, Los Angeles

Juana Maria Rodriguez
Graduate student in Ethnic Studies,
University of California, Berkeley

James Ruppert
Department of Native Studies,
University of Alaska

Alan R. Velie
Department of English,
University of Oklahoma

Gerald Vizenor (Chippewa)
Department of Native American Studies,
University of California, Berkeley

Robert Allen Warrior (Osage)
Department of English,
Stanford University

Index